Preaching Through Proverbs: A Collection of Sermons by the Pastors of Central Africa

Published by WalkwithGod.com.
Text Copyright © 2018 by WalkwithGod.com

Cover photo courtesy of Craig Thompson © 2017.

Printed in the USA.
First printing.
ISBN: 978-1-64407-000-0

"Wisdom is better than weapons of war."
Ecclesiastes 9:18a

Table of Contents

Introduction

In the Fall of 2017, I was privileged visit Lusaka to teach the book of Proverbs at a biannual training for pastors, teachers and church leaders from the four central African countries of Malawi, Mozambique, Zambia and Zimbabwe. This was my second term with the students. During this intensive time of teaching, the students were responsible for digging into the scripture and developing sermons which they would be able to use as soon as they returned home.

This book is one result of their work. Each of them has written commentary on scripture, provided illustrations to go with the sermons and included questions to ask an audience. Most of the sermons have a "target audience" to help further contextualize the message of Proverbs for these groups. Also included are the personal reflections which the students wrote about how the book of Proverbs has impacted their lives. A big applause to these wonderful women and men of God who sacrifice so much to invest into their biblical education.

I hope that these sermons and lessons inspire you in your own preparation. Some of the stories are personal and true. Some are parables. The questions can be simple and straightforward at times and very soul-searching at others.

The book is laid out in a simple format. Each author is listed alphabetically by last name followed by his or her sermons. Because there are a variety of primary languages spoken by the students, my task has been to take the sermons and edit them in such a way that the original words, idioms and sentence structure are used (as much as possible) while endeavoring to present the material as a grammatically cohesive unit. On a few occasions, I edited for content or theological integrity to the Scripture.

The following people crowd-sourced the typing of these sermons and really made this book possible by shortening the amount of time I would have had to spend on it if I were doing it all by myself. I extend a very heartfelt thanks to each of them:

Kamie Beeson, Michelle Chapman, Noelle Coleman, Kayci Glasgow, Tsavo Glasgow, Charlotte Hallman, Mandy Jackson, Sandra Monday, Anna Thompson, Deana Thompson, Petra Thompson and Cindy Williams. My dear friend Mikey G. personally asked several typists to participate.

I want to extend thanks to Jürgen Rudolph, Director of Education in Africa for Church of God World Missions, for the opportunity to teach in Africa. Jürgen is a true servant of Jesus Christ who embodies the devotion of Christ to build the kingdom of God regardless of obstacles or personal attacks.

Thank you to all of the people who have generously given money to support the trips we take for evangelism and training. Thank you also to those who gave generously to support the production of this book.

My wife, Deana, is my companion of many years. She keeps the home running (no small task!). She took time out of her busy schedule to lend her editing skills to the final copy. (All errors remain mine!) Thank you for encouraging me to keep fulfilling the calling on my life! I love you.

Final thanks go to Jesus who enabled me and counted me faithful, putting me into the ministry. One day I'll see you face to face!

Craig Thompson

Abel C. Chewe

Abel C. Chewe (1965) is a full time Pastor at Bethel Worship Center in Zanimuone, Zambia. He graduated from Luwingu High School in 1983 (Grade 12). He also holds an Advanced Diploma of Pastoral Leadership from AFMIM Leadership Institute (2010). He has worked with Mutual Medical Aid Service as a Marketing Officer (2006-2009). In 1985, Abel married his beautiful wife Delphister with whom he has seven children and two grandchildren. His hobbies include cooking, having fun, watching football and reading books. His favorite verse is 1 Samuel 12:23. His advice to young ministers is as follows: "The measure of ministry is sacrifice. They need to sacrifice their time, energy, and money as well as their life. They have to earn the respect of the elders by setting themselves as an example in their speech, life, love, faith and purity. They have to live so others can see Christ in them. They should expect of others only what they expect of themselves. They must develop their expectations of others with considerations of their skills, maturity, and experience; and they need to be patient with distracted or slow learners. They are to monitor their expectations of others. They are to clarify their expectations of others. They have to end with encouragement; people love to be thanked for a job well done."

Principles for Being Generous

Proverbs 3:27-28; 29:7,13; 25:21; Isaiah 58:7;
Matthew 5:42; Luke 12:33; Romans 12:13

Audience: Congregation and Business Owners

Isaiah 58:7   The Bible teaches about acting with kindness, charity, justice and generosity. This truly is pleasing to God.

Matthew 5:42   The Bible teaches us to help those who are in need. It is more important to give justice and mercy than to receive it.

Luke 12:33 In this verse, the Bible teaches us that money seen as an end in itself quickly traps us and cuts us off from both God and the need.

Romans 12:13 Here the Bible teaches us to practice hospitality and to share what we have, even if it is little.

Proverbs 25:21 The Bible encourages us to share not only with those who love us but more especially with those who seem to be our enemies.

Proverbs 22:9; 11:24-25 These verses present a paradox. We become richer by being generous. The world says to hold onto as much as possible, but God blesses those who give freely of their possessions, time, and energy.   When we give, God supplies us with more so that we can give more. In addition, giving helps us gain a right perspective on our possessions. We realize that they were never really ours to begin with but they were given to us by God to be used to help others.

Illustration

What happened to me in 1998 was that in this year I went with my uncle to Lake Bangweulu to buy fish. When we travelled 48 km, I fell sick. My uncle decided to dump me in the hands of unknown people. Likely enough, those people helped me so much. They gave me some medicine, and I spent a night with them. The next morning, I felt much better, and I was encouraged to go now to my uncle. I started off around 0600 hours and reached the place at 1400 hours the same day.

When I was going around, I found my uncle who dumped me. Unfortunately, he had run out of money. The people wanted to kill him because he had failed to pay the people he hired for a boat. I decided also not to assist him, but God spoke to me that if I did not pay for him, I would contribute to his death. I paid for him, and he was released from their hands.

Questions

1. Does God's love touch your wallet?
2. Does your money free you to help others?
3. How would your life be different if you lived the way Jesus sets forth in this passage?

Remember that if God's love touches your wallet, money frees you to help others. You are storing up lasting treasures in heaven.

Living with Integrity
Proverbs 3:33-35; 10:3,19,22,24-25; 11:21,27,30-31; 24:8-9

Audience: Mixed congregation

In Proverbs 10:3,9,22,24-25, the Bible describes God's care for the godly. Being godly doesn't mean being like God in the sense of being perfect. Obviously, that is impossible for human beings. Godly people are those who love the Lord and are seeking to follow him (Psalm 4:3). As Christians, we have been given the power of the Holy Spirit to help us live godly lives (2 Peter 1:3). We must choose to either reject God and live our own way or accept God and follow Him.

Proverbs 11:21,27,30-31; 3:33-35 One of the greatest resources God gives us is family. Family provides acceptance, encouragement, guidance and council. Bringing trouble on your family, whether through anger or through an exaggerated desire for independence, is foolish because you cut yourself off from all they provide.

In your family, strive for healing, communication, and understanding. A wise person is a model of a meaningful life. Like a tree attracts people to its shade, a wise person's sense of purpose attracts others who want to know how they, too, can find meaning. Gaining wisdom for yourself can be the first step in leading people to God.

Contrary to popular opinion, no one sins and gets away with it. The righteous are rewarded for their faith. The wicked are punished for their sins. Don't think for a moment that "it won't matter," or "nobody will know," or "we won't get caught."

Living with Integrity
Proverbs 18:3; 19:29; 22:8; 26:1,3,27; 28:18

Proverbs 18:3 The Bible teaches us that the righteous man leads a blameless life. It is far more valuable than wealth, but most people don't act as if they believe in this. We are to live as men who are representing God, not our own interests. That is integrity.

Proverbs 19:29 A man of integrity should not be a mocker or a crook. He/she must be upright with morals.

Proverbs 22:8 The Bible tells us always to follow God's Word instead of hearsay. We are to trust what God's Word says rather than what someone claims is true. That is integrity.

Proverbs 26:1,3,27 People cannot honor a person who has dishonored himself through his/her actions. We must believe that God's way is better than our own. That's integrity.

Proverbs 28:18 The Bible says that the blameless will be rescued from harm, but the crooked will be suddenly destroyed. As servants of God, we are to lead people away from unjust proceedings. That is integrity.

Living with Integrity
Proverbs 15:26; 21:8,12; Psalm 41:12; Proverbs 11:3, 19:1, 20:7

Proverbs 19:1 The Bible teaches us that a blameless life is far more valuable than wealth, but most people don't act as if they believe this. Afraid of not getting everything they want, they will pay any price to increase their wealth—cheating on their taxes, stealing from stores or employers, withholding tithes, refusing to give. But when we know and love God, we realize that a lower standard of living, or even poverty, is a small price to pay for personal integrity.

Do your actions show that you sacrifice your integrity to increase your wealth? What changes do you want to make in order to get your priorities straight?

As men/children of God, we should be responsible and concerned and honest. God's work is better accomplished by devoted people. Everyone's energy is needed to carry out God's work.

Living with Integrity
Proverbs 24:8-9, 13:6, 16:7; 17:13

Planning to do evil can be as wrong as doing it, because what you think determines what you will do. Left unchecked, wrong desires will lead us to sin. God wants pure hearts, free from sin, and planning evil brings sinful thoughts into your mind. Should you say, "Then I might as well go ahead and do it because I have already planned it"? No. You have sinned in your attitude, but you have not yet harmed other people. Stop in your tracks and ask God to forgive you and put you on a different path. Blameless living safeguards your life. Every choice for good sets into motion other opportunities for good. Evil choices follow the same pattern, but in the opposite direction. Each decision you make to obey God's Word will bring a greater sense of order to your life, while each decision to disobey will bring confusion and destruction. The right choice you make reflects your integrity.

Extra scriptures on the topic: Proverbs 14:14,22; 29:10; 21:8,12,16,21; 2 Chronicles 18:2-3,25-26,28

As a person who has integrity, you need to see to it that everything you are doing is approved by God through the Word of God and do what it says correctly, not what people want us to do for them. It does us no good to seek God's advice if we ignore it when it is given. When we have integrity, we are to make sure that whatever we are doing is what God wants us to do. We should take God's Word as our standard of living. That is integrity.

An Unhealthy Tongue

Proverbs 10:8; 11:12-13; 12:18-19,22; 16:27-28; 17:9,14,19-20; 18:9,20-21; 19:5,22; 20:3,19; 21:6; 22:10; 25:23; 26:2,20-22; 28:18; 28:23; 29:5

Commentary

Proverbs 10:8   By hating another person, you become a liar or a fool. If you try to conceal your hatred, you end up lying. If you slander the other person and are proven wrong, you are a fool. The only way out is to admit your hateful feelings to God. Ask him to change your heart and to help you love instead of hate.

Proverbs 11:12-13   We should not harm our friends through careless talking. You may end up doing a great harm to your neighbor.

Proverbs 12:18-19,22   Godly people find life because they live life more fully each day. They also find life because people usually live longer when they live right.

Proverbs 16:27-28   The Bible teaches us not to be troublemakers or peace breakers. As children of God, we are to be friendly with everyone because jealousies can keep the church from growing. Holiness is coupled with living in peace. We must pursue peace as we become more like Christ.

Proverbs 17:9,14,19-20   These Proverbs are saying that we should be willing to disregard the faults of others. Forgiving faults is necessary to any relationship. It is tempting, especially in an argument, to bring up all the mistakes the other person has ever made. Love, however, keeps its mouth shut.

Proverbs 18:9,20-21   Here the Bible teaches us to master self-control of what you say. Words can cut and destroy. James recognized this truth when he stated, "The tongue is a flame of fire; it is a whole world of wickedness" (James 3:16). We are to stop and think before reacting.

Proverbs 19:5,22 Destructive gossip causes problems. Even if you do not initiate a lie, you become responsible if you pass it along. We are not to circulate rumors.

Proverbs 20:3,19 The Bible teaches us that a resourceful person can find a way out of a fight and avoid retaliation. Foolish people find it impossible to avoid strife. Men and women of character can. What kind of a person are you? Talking about every little irritation and piece of gossip only keeps the fire of anger going. Refusing to discuss it then cuts the fuel line and makes the fire die out. Does someone continually irritate you? Decide not to complain about the person and see if your irritation dies from lack of fuel.

Proverbs 21:6 The Bible here teaches us that lying to one another disrupts unity by destroying trust. It tears down relationships and may lead to serious conflict in a church, family, or at our workplace. We are not to exaggerate statistics, pass out rumors and gossip, or say things to build up our own image. Be committed to telling the truth.

Proverbs 22:10 The Bible encourages us not to promote quarrels and foolish arguments. Selfishness can ruin a church, but genuine humility can build it. Treat others with common courtesy.

Proverbs 25:23 We are to straighten our lives before God. We must live differently from unbelievers, not letting secular society dictate how to treat others. Do not let your brother become angry because of your gossip. It hurts.

Proverbs 26:2,20-22 The Bible teaches us to avoid evil speaking against our fellow believers and non-believers. While avoiding these wrongs, we must also let God's Word show us the standard by which to live.

Proverbs 28:18 A sinner's conscience will drive him to either guilt, resulting in repentance, or to death itself because of a refusal to repent. It is not an act of kindness to try to make him feel better. The more guilt he feels, the more likely he is to turn to God and repent. If we interfere with the natural consequences of his actions, we may make it easier for him to continue sinning.

Proverbs 28:23 God does not overlook lies, flattery, deception, or boasting. Each of these sins originates from a bad attitude that is eventually expressed in our speech. The tongue can be our greatest enemy because, though small, it can do greater damage (James 3:5-6). Be careful how you use yours.

Proverbs 29:5 It is disgusting to hear a person butter up someone. Flattery is phony, and it covers up a person's real intentions. Christians should not be flatterers. Those who proclaim that God is truth have a special responsibility to be honest.

Are you honest and straightforward in your words and actions? Or do you tell people what they want to hear in order to get what you want or to get ahead? What are you doing about this situation in order to bring peace? Remember that sin always blocks our vision of God. If we want to see God, we must renounce the sins of flattering or of tearing down our fellow Christian. We must obey God.

Personal Reflection

I have come to understand that the tongue (my speech) is very powerful. The tongue can pollute and poison. What I say really reflects what is in my heart. God is speaking to me that I should change the way I speak and start speaking things which can bless my fellow believers without hurting them. My biggest challenge is that on my own, I cannot do anything without the help of the Holy Spirit. God is telling me to change my behavior. He is telling me to practice listening before speaking, ponder the proper response (if any), to place my hand over my mouth, to put my words to the test, and to prepare my tongue with my heart (Proverbs 16:23) whether to speak and what to speak.

I should use my tongue to edify and build my friends, not criticize and destroy. I should set myself to be an example for others in speech in order to do the right thing. I will allow the Holy Spirit to control my tongue. God is telling me to change. I must learn not to say too much or too little and to say the right thing at the right time.

The big issue I am facing in my church is gossiping. Members are quarreling all the time. Now I have learned how to sort out these issues of gossiping. Today I have come to understand that the tongue controlled by the Holy Spirit produces speech which is consistent with the character of Christ in us. The Scripture addresses what to do to make the church to sustain. People must practice listening before speaking and pick their words carefully. People should pare their words to the minimum and put their words to the test, because the quickest way for believers to confirm or contradict his/her profession of faith in Christ is by what he/she says.

Daniel Chitondwe

Daniel Chitondwe lives in Mutare, Zimbabwe where he is the Assistant Pastor at Greenside Miracle Tabernacle. He has been with the church for almost 30 years and is actively involved with the youth ministry. After teaching the youth about the wisdom from the book of Proverbs, he has seen changes in their behavior and conduct and in how they are participating in the work of the church.

Mother's Leadership Lessons
Proverbs 31:1-9

Audience: Business Owners

Proverbs 31:1,2,8,9   This is the introduction of the words of wisdom from a mother to her son. This son was a King and was called King Lemuel. In 31:2, the mother is not happy with what she is seeing or hearing of what her son is doing. She is emphasizing her disappointment and the pain of giving birth to this son. In 31:8, the mother is trying to spread this message to all those who appear not to know and who show ignorance. In 31:9, she is telling them to exercise their authority by teaching and making correct judgments which help the poor and needy or those who cannot stand for themselves

Proverbs 31:3   This verse talks about the mother advising the child not to womanize, that is to have women outside his own wife. He cannot concentrate with these types of women. Women have a tendency of disturbing the work of kings or leaders. In this case, to the business owners, I remind you that your mind can be distracted by paying more attention to women (not your wife) than to the business.

Proverbs 31:4   During this period, when Solomon wrote this book, wine or strong drinks were given to people dying, those with stress or those people in pain. This was meant for them to forget or to ease the pain. Now the mother is advising or giving wise words to us sons or business owners not to participate in drinking or taking wine as it doesn't solve any problems related to our business. Alcohol can disturb the mind and can lead to injustice and poor decisions. Leaders have better things to do than to anesthetize themselves with wine.

Proverbs 31:5 The verse tells us that even if the dying people drink wine, it doesn't solve or help anything. Rather it brings more problems than solving issues.

Proverbs 31:6 According to the contextual meaning, people with pain and stress were given wine. This was meant to release pain. It was used as a drug to ease pain or to release stress. If the wine is taken in excess, it means people will get drunk. This will disturb the leaders or business owners and lead to the paralysis of the operations.

Proverbs 31:7 People or leaders can be encouraged to drink and forget their poverty, but that won't solve anything. The trouble will remain unresolved. Misery can be forgotten, but it's a temporary setback.

Illustration

There was a business man who had his shop which he used to run together with his wife. He used to not drink beer. Due to the type of friends he engaged, he began to drink beer. Due to drinking, he began to lose control of himself. Then he grew to love a worker within his shop. Because he did not want his wife to know about this, he asked his wife to stay at home. He remained alone at the business. By doing that, each time he got drunk he could come to his work place and take his worker from work and drive out.

This started to disturb the operations of the business. Some co-workers discovered that their boss was going out with their fellow worker. Due to excess drinking of alcohol, he would come to the business and disturb everyone. The workers started to show no respect. The standard deteriorated, and the customers began to shame the place.

As the business owner, he began to lack the values of a business man. As events unfolded, the workers had no respect for the business owner. He ended up broke, and the business was closed. This was due to the practice of drinking beer at the work place and falling in love with a worker after being drunk. He made wrong decisions, and other workers took advantage of his state when he was drunk. He also created debts which he failed to pay.

Questions
1. How should a business owner solve stressful issues at his business (e.g. paying debts and paying salaries on time)?
2. Does drinking wine affect the decision making at a business? If yes, how?
3. How does a wise business owner advise other fellow business owners?

Wisdom Personified
Proverbs 8:5,6,8-9

Audience: Mixed congregation

Wisdom is portrayed as a woman who guides us. In Proverbs 8:5, these are the blessings of wisdom being executed by a woman to guide us as wisdom occupies us. To the simple ones, meaning those people who don't want to reason things which are simple to understand, they must learn to be wise in a way of caution and provision. To fools, meaning people who do not listen, they should take heed from what the woman tells or advises us congregants.

Proverbs 8:6 Here the woman is stressing the need to pay attention to her. She is emphasizing that what she says is of importance, and what comes from her mouth is of great benefit. The words from her mouth will guide us.

Proverbs 8:8 In this context, the woman is telling us that each word of wisdom is right before the Lord. The Lord does not fool or tell lies. People who listen to the word of wisdom will benefit, because nothing wisdom says is unfounded. It will be the truth.

Proverbs 8:9 Here it is said that those who listen to the wise words and believe in them will have a good and undoubted life. Their life will be straight and without questions.

Illustration
When children, youth, and men & women in a congregation are being taught or advised, they must take heed to what is being taught. Normally, wise words are not taken seriously, and people fall by the wayside. Women are at times not taken seriously when they speak words of wisdom.

One day a woman from our church taught about tithes and offerings. She was mainly targeting business people. It so happened that I was one of the businessmen who was attending the service. She stressed on the importance of paying tithes, and she said that tithing is a law which should not be tampered with. She gave examples of other businessmen who took heed to paying tithes and stated that their businesses were blessed. I ignored her teaching, and I spent the whole year not paying tithes. The results were seen later when my business began to crumble and to deteriorate. I didn't listen to the wise words from this woman. The moment I realized that mistake of not paying tithes and I began to pay, my business began to grow.

Questions

1. Why do people in general look down upon women when they teach?
2. Why does God at times use women to deliver words of wisdom?
3. What happens if one obeys the words of wisdom?

Wisdom Personified
Proverbs 8:27-28

Wisdom was present at the creation and works with the Creator. In Proverbs 8:27, wisdom tells us that when heaven was created, she was present. In Genesis 11, when God created the heavens and the earth, wisdom was present to give guidance. In Genesis 1:2 wisdom was also present when darkness was over the face of the deep. God used wisdom to choose what to start with so that things could have order.

Proverbs 8:28 When the sea was created and separated from the land in Genesis 1:6, the presence of wisdom was there. Wisdom was very important to make the creation successful.

Illustration

Genesis 1:1 says, "In the beginning, God created the heavens and the earth." This tells us that for God to think of making or creating the heavens and the earth, He used wisdom to do so. When wisdom is applied, all things will be in order. We are told in Genesis 1:2 that, "the earth was without form and void." It means nothing was properly arranged as it is today. He used wisdom (1:3) to declare things to start to appear on the earth. We are taught that each time we listen and follow what wisdom wants, we will be successful and will prosper just as God Himself who used it. Today the whole world is happy and enjoying the created world. God Himself provides wisdom to those who are prepared to accept it.

Questions

1. If wisdom was not used in the creation, how do you think the world was going to be created?
2. What does it mean that wisdom is the foundation of life?
3. How does God provide wisdom?

Wisdom Personified
Proverbs 8:19-20,22-24,26-31

Proverbs 8:19-20 In verse 19 Solomon is saying that if wisdom is upon you, the riches in the world are with you. All the respect you desire is found in wisdom. For one to get rich, he or she has to be wise. You can easily acquire a lot of wealth, meaning properties and possession. But only someone who is wise can really have the fruit of wisdom. There are fruits of wisdom, benefits. People take gold as very precious, but here Solomon is saying that wisdom is more important or precious than gold. One can walk ahead with the righteous if he possesses wisdom.

Proverbs 8:22-24 God says wisdom is primary and fundamental. It is the foundation on which all life is built. This is also alluded to by Paul and John by describing the presence of Christ. The foundation is wisdom. Houses are built on a strong foundation. If the foundation is weak, the house won't last and will fall. Therefore, a Christian must build his Christian life on a strong foundation with wisdom. One needs to be wise.

Proverbs 8:26-31 Wisdom is God's delightful tool. There are lots of benefits in wisdom. Wisdom requires attention. Many are happy when they reap what they sow. Wisdom has benefitted those who walk, live, and eat with it. Even at school, children have benefitted from wisdom. Heaven and earth were a result of the presence of wisdom.

Illustration

There is a woman who recently took Jesus as her personal Savior. She has a business which was left to her by her husband who died of cancer. When she came to church, I taught her how she should live as a Christian. I told her of the benefits of being wise, that is to know friends to partner with since she is a single mother. She followed that advice. She left all her old friends, and she got God-fearing women as new friends. She took wisdom as her foundation in her business. As I speak, she is leading a God-fearing life and is prospering so well with her family.

Questions
1. How do you apply wisdom as a foundation to your life?
2. How does wisdom prove to bring benefits in a Christian life?
3. How do Christians without wisdom behave?

Wisdom Personified

Proverbs 8:17-19

Audience: Mixed congregation

Wisdom produces lots of benefits.

Proverbs 8:17 Here wisdom is telling us that she loves those who love her, meaning that without us loving or having the law in our hearts, she won't come to our hearts as well. We need to show her that we want her most. We have the desire for her to enter our hearts first. For those who are really serious, those who are thirsty, those who seek her, and those who work very hard for God's kingdom, she will take the time to show up. The one who seeks her will find her waiting. God approves those who listen to wisdom.

Proverbs 8:18 Here wisdom is trying to tell us that those who want to be rich and to be respected (i.e. to be counted among others) should get it from her. Wealth is good welfare, prosperity, good well-being, happiness, joy, and valuable materials. These are only gotten by people who have wisdom. Also, holiness, purity and being upright — that is, to live a life which pleases God — is only obtained in her. So in wisdom you can live the way God wants, and you will benefit by living well.

Proverbs 8:19 Gold is regarded as a very precious mineral, and so is silver. Here, Solomon is valuing the fruit, which is the product of wisdom, as very precious. It helps us better than the earthly minerals. The value of wisdom is greater than any mineral found on this earth, meaning that if one obtains wisdom, he or she will be very rich and will be counted among others.

Illustration

My daddy is the third born in a family of eight members. Out of all the members, he is the only one who is a born again Christian.

He is somebody who fears God, and he worships God like nobody's business! He loves doing the work of God very much. Because of this background, wisdom found its home in him. He is now 75 years old. He now has a lot of wealth in the form of three houses, a business which has a building worth millions of dollars, and four modern vehicles. Recently, he was chosen to be the Provincial Overseer of Manicaland Province, North in Mutare, Zimbabwe. All these are a result of the wisdom he has which is producing these benefits. He is living a holy life, a life which God is wanting. He is leading a righteous life, a life which is pleasing God. He is benefiting from the presence of wisdom in him. All the other family members think he uses Juju to acquire all his wealth, but that is not the case. These are the works of God. These are the fruits of allowing wisdom to take control.

Questions
1. What does wisdom do if one loves and seeks her diligently?
2. Where do we find riches, honor, wealth and righteousness?
3. What does one do to have a righteous life?

Wisdom Personified
Proverbs 8:32-36

Audience: Mixed congregation

Wisdom needs to be paid attention to. We should listen to her. Proverbs 8:32-33 Solomon is explaining that those people who pay attention to wisdom are blessed. All that they desire will prosper. Wisdom gives instructions. Those who obey them will be wiser and wiser. Listening pays a lot of dividends. Some ignore the word of wisdom from God, and they normally fall by the wayside. God wants people who are obedient.

Proverbs 8:34 Here the Bible is telling us that a lot of blessings are found only by those who listen to the word of wisdom. People should always watch every day at the gate of wisdom to see, because that's the entrance point. They need to wait for wisdom by the door. One needs to catch or grab wisdom when she comes out from the doors and the gates. Attention is needed always. One needs to be watchful.

Proverbs 8:35-36 Here Solomon is finalizing the results of paying attention or listening. Life is the entire living of a human being. This means that whosoever has wisdom and is wise will live a good, happy life, a life full of benefits, a life full of wealth and honor. God grants everything to someone with wisdom. Those who do not have wisdom always injure themselves. Dying is easy to those who do not like to be wise.

Illustration

I have an older sister. One day she told me that she was moving from the church she was at to another. This church is led by a "prophet" named Makandiwa. I advised her not to join that church. The reasons were that, in my opinion, (a) the church loves money better than anything else and (b) the church has false doctrines. Each time they go to church, they have to pay a lot of money, to the extent of submitting all of her salary. Prayer requests were to be accompanied with huge sums of money.

She began to borrow money from people and took a loan from her work so that she could pay the money to the so-called "man of God." She sold most of her property in order to clear her debts. Her prayer requests were never answered. What she wanted was never achieved. As I write, she is regretting that she did not listen to my advice. If she had listened to the wise advice which I gave her, she would not be in this position. I advised her to go before the Lord to seek guidance, but she did not pay attention. Now she is crying because she has nothing.

Questions
1. How do you deal with or assist people who don't pay attention to the word of wisdom?
2. What are the results of failing to listen to God?
3. Does God forgive those who don't listen to his Word?

Personal Reflection
Through the Scriptures from Proverbs chapter 8, God is teaching me personally that when I allow the wisdom of God to lead and show me direction, I will have many blessings. Following wisdom will make me a good, blessed somebody. Wisdom in this chapter is like a human being or a person. This means that I should listen to her because it pays to listen. I have also learned that I should depend on wisdom and trust it. All my plans will come right if I trust wisdom. Also, as Pastor of my church, I should allow wisdom to use me in counseling and even preaching. When I return home, I will work very hard to teach wisdom to people, especially this very basic book of Proverbs. I will preach and teach it regularly. Families will be given assignments to make sure they learn and practice it at home. To the community, I will organize some seminars with the local chancellors so that I will have the chance to teach people of the community.

Giving and Accepting Counsel

Proverbs 3:1,2; 9:7-9; 11:14; 12:15; 13:1,13;
15:22,31; 20:18; 24:5-6; 25:12; 27:5-6,17

Commentary

Proverbs 3:1-2 These verse reveal that Solomon is telling his son to keep whatever he is going to be told. The son is pleaded with to accept the commandments and not to forget the teachings. As long as he lives he has to always remember the teachings from his father.

Proverbs 9:7-9 Here we have two classes: the mocker and the wise person. One can be identified by the way he or she responds to criticism. Instead of tossing back a quick putdown or clever retort when rebuked, listen to what is being said. Learn from your critics. This is the path of a wise man. Wisdom starts with knowing God. He gives insight into living because He created life. We need to know God better and better.

Proverbs 11:14 Solomon is saying a good leader needs to use wiser advisers. A person's perspective and understanding is severely limited. He or she may not have all the facts or may be blinded by bias, emotions, or wrong impressions. To be a wise leader at home, at church, or at work, one needs to seek the counsel of others and to be open to their advice. A decision can be considered.

Proverbs 12:15 Here we see a person who doesn't want to be advised. Someone says, "I am never wrong. I am always right." This is an attitude. A man can tell other people that they are foolish when he doesn't realize that he himself is a fool. A wise man listens to advice from others.

Proverbs 13:1,13 A wise son listens to what his father tells him, but a lazy person or son doesn't listen when advised or taught. He won't accept advice. God created us, knows us, and loves us. It only makes sense that we listen to his instructions and do what he says. If you obey God's instructions, you will run right and find His kind of power to live. If you ignore them, you will have breakdowns, accidents, and failures.

Proverbs 15:22,31 People with tunnel vision, those who are locked into one way of thinking, are likely to miss the right road because they have closed their minds to any new options. We need the help of those who can enlarge our vision and broaden our perspective. Seek out the advice of those who know you and who have a wealth of experience. Build a network of advisers. One should be open to new ideas and be willing to weigh their suggestions carefully.

Proverbs 20:18 Any plans being arranged should be a result of counseling. There should be guidance. This means that all plans must be advised.

Proverbs 24:5-6 An athlete who thinks, who assesses the situation and plans strategies, has an advantage over a physically stronger but unthinking opponent. Wisdom, not muscle, is certainly why God has put people in charge of the animal kingdom. We exercise regularly and eat well to build strength, but we don't take equal pains to develop wisdom. It is not a sign of weakness to ask for advice. Instead, it is so foolish not to ask for it. Find good advisors before making any big decision. They can help you expand your evaluation choices.

Proverbs 25:12 This is listening with a view to obedience. When one hears, he should be in a position to do or to follow the instructions.

Proverbs 27:5-6,17 A friend who has your best interests at heart may have to give you unpleasant advice at times, but you know it is for your own good. An enemy, by contrast, may whisper sweet words and happily send you on your way to ruin. A friend's advice, no matter how painful, is much better. There is a mental sharpness that comes from being around good people.

A meeting of minds can help people see their ideas with new clarity, refine them and shape them into brilliant insights. This requires discussion partners who can challenge each other and stimulate thought, people who focus on the idea without involving their egos in the discussion, people who know how to attack the thought and not the thinker. Two friends who bring their ideas together can help each other become sharper.

Personal Reflection

God is telling me to listen to what wisdom is saying to my life. A lot has been happening within my family and business. God sometimes visits me through dreams. My wife in most cases is shown by God what or how we should solve our challenges. I at times do not listen to her. But after going through this module and the verses I read, I have learned to always remember the teachings of my parents. Accept advice from my wife. Before I do my final decision, I need to counsel with my wife. At times, I need to find out from God before I make decisions. The biggest challenge has been that sometimes I would look down upon what my wife advised me. I need to take her seriously and work with her together. God is telling me to change my behavior. I have learned a lot, and from now on I will work a new life that is led by wisdom. I will be wiser through the years or as life takes a new twist. There are not many obstacles in obeying God, but I need to be more serious. I am going to fast and pray to God to give me strength and wisdom.

As for my family, there is a problem of looking down on each other. I will call for a prayer for all my family members. With wisdom from God, I will ask each member to learn and listen and obey what God says through respecting each other and respect the decisions done and sent by God. At my local church, most people don't believe when I teach and preach. But I am happy God is revealing Himself. A lot more people who are serious and who listen to advice from God as I am teaching are improving their lives, and their lives are changing. We are going to use more testimonies from the congregation. This will make others start to realize the importance of the teachings.

To my community, I would encourage people to go to church and worship their God and listen to what the Lord says about their lives. I would also ask them to make good decisions before making them final.

To the nation, I would like the leaders to consult the Lord on how to improve the economy of the nation. A lot of wisdom is necessary, and they need to take advice from those who are always before the Lord.

 WalkwithGod.com Publishing

Tichaona Dhina

Tichaona Dhina (1978) lives in Mutare, Zimbabwe. He has been involved in ministry for three years and works in youth ministry in a rural area called Buhera. He has 11 years of experience in construction. His favorite hobby is football. Tichaona is married to one wife and has five children. His favorite verse is John 14:23. The advice which he offers to young ministers is, "Beware of false teachers. Always refer to the Word of God."

Selfishness
Proverbs 1:8,11,13,15,19; 10:4

Audience: Teenagers

In 1:8 is the instruction of a leader to a teenager who has started the path of selfishness. Instruct teenagers to submit themselves to their parents. As for the parents, they should give good instructions and love to their children.

In 1:11, the leader is informing teenagers to have good friends. The other friends were not aware of their way of living. We are warned against taking the blood of the innocent.

In 1:13, the leader instructs the teenager not to have precious goods without work. Wealth gotten easily is temptation. Also, avoid the path of these kinds of people.

In 1:15, the leader instructs teenagers not to stay or move with evil friends. The leader is equipping teenagers to withdraw from their bad path. He reminds them to have knowledge about their way.

In 1:19, the leader outlines the harvest of selfishness of teenagers. He mentions the final results of finding wealth easily. The final reward of selfishness is death.

Proverbs 10:4 The leader advises youth to be hard workers as the way to prosperity. He also states that the result of slack hands is the way to poverty. It is a sign of wisdom when you are working.

Illustration
It was when I was a teenager 17 years ago, our pastor was always teaching us to obey our parents. He encouraged us to start

projects as youths as a way to get money in good and godly ways. There was one boy in our youth team named Tinto. He was a lazy boy. He was always against our Pastor. He was simply mean, and he was a selfish boy. Tinto was starting to smoke and use drugs and was not sleeping at home. The boy increased in selfishness and became a big thief.

One day they were in their business of robbing and theft. It was the end of the month, and they knew the workers were paid their salaries. They took their weapons during night hours and were awaiting workers who came late from work. As they were waiting as thieves, they found a man who was moving along the road. The team robbed the man, and the man was beaten to death.

Then Tinto and his company shared the money and clothes. Tinto was given a jacket. After their business was done, they went to their homes.

The following day when Tinto was up, his mother told him that his father had not come home that night. He began to feel bad. When he looked, he saw that he had been given his father's jacket. He totally knew he had killed his father.

Finally, he surrendered himself to the police. He was charged, found guilty and sentenced to 150 years which is life in jail. These are the results of selfishness.

1. Why is easy wealth a temptation?
2. What is the difference between selfishness and wisdom?
3. Why is wisdom important for teenagers?

Products of a Healthy Tongue

Proverbs 10:21,32; 17:28

Audience: Business Owners

This lesson is about how you benefit from a healthy tongue according to the scriptures. It shows that when you are righteous, you know which words to use. Some words are not fitted to business owners, because there are different characteristics of languages from many peoples.

In Proverbs 10:21,32 we find that lips of righteousness contribute to riches. We need to be righteous. This can give your lips the ability to talk with every person. In business, we can purchase credits or even loans. If you have an unhealthy tongue, you fail and your business goes downhill.

In 10:21, this verse is indicating that when you are righteous, your lips are able to produce greater things and prosperity in your life. In 10:32, the verse is inviting our lips to select words as the products of wisdom and not to be like the wicked who speak perverse things.

Again in 17:28, this gives advice to business owners not to speak every word we feel like speaking. The person who holds his peace is counted wise and understanding. The word gives us wisdom by telling us that even if you are foolish, if you hold your peace, by this you are counted as wise and esteemed as being a person of understanding.

Illustration

Mr. Jimmy is a business owner in our community. He is a great man, a righteous man who is able to serve every person. He is able to serve people from many different customs and backgrounds because of his good lips. Some people think he has some type of miracle power. However, he is the example of wisdom which is displayed in a healthy tongue.

Questions
1. How do a person's lips cause troubles in business?
2. Is a healthy tongue connected with wisdom?
3. Why are business owners advised to use a healthy tongue?

Life Through a Healthy Tongue
Proverbs 10:11; 18:4

Audience: Congregation

This sermon is about life that comes from a healthy tongue according to the scriptures. Scripture advises the congregation to control their tongue, as life come from it. The scriptures inform the congregation that in the mouth are deep waters and the wellspring of wisdom. This means we must use our mouth with diligence, for it is the expression of wisdom.

Through a healthy tongue, life is connected, for every good word comes from a healthy tongue. This can multiply the number of days in your life. If we want to live many days, have many friends, stay out of troubles and see the church multiply, a healthy tongue is needed.

Proverbs 10:11 This verse indicates that the mouth of a person who applies wisdom is the pipeline of good life which is acceptable to God.

Proverbs 18:4 promotes the mouth as the source of good life. A healthy tongue produces a life which is sweet like honey for its owner.

Illustration

There is a congregation which was not connected to the wisdom of life. The church was not aware of the scriptures on healthy tongues. Instead of using their mouth to acknowledge God, they started to talk about each other. The church was divided, because some were producing false stories about others.

One day as they were in the church, the pastor was preaching not the Word of God but preaching what he wanted to say to the people. A fight started, and the church was broken up. This story teaches us that when you are not aware of your mouth, you can destroy an entire congregation.

Questions
1. Are all words good for a congregation?
2. What type of congregation do you want to be part of?
3. What are the benefits of a healthy tongue in the congregation?

A Healthy Tongue
Proverbs 15:1-2; 16:23

Audience: Women

This sermon is going to discuss about women who live with unbelieving husbands in their home. Proverbs 15:1-2 shows that when any discussion applies grievous words, it automatically becomes an uncontrolled discussion which will only lead to more wrath.

By so doing a woman with an unbelieving husband should be aware of her mouth when she is talking or discussing with her husband. Most of their husbands are drunks. Others come home moneyless from their jobs, again with a lot of noise.

So it is the duty of yours as a mother to use your heart to teach knowledge to your mouth to produce healthy tongues as the way to control wrath.

Illustration
In our community, there is a woman who is a believer who is married to a drunk. One day her husband came without money on pay day. He was very drunk. As he got home, his wife told him not to drink anything, not even water. Since they had no money, the man killed himself. Now she is a widow because of an unhealthy tongue.

Proverbs 15:1-2 teaches us the truth that when someone answers with a soft answer it turns away wrath.

Proverbs 16:23 reminds us that it simply gives light to the heart to check your words before they come out. Teach your heart not to speak out every word which passes through your mind.

Questions

1. Why does the mouth produce things (feelings/emotions) in the heart?
2. Are all words from the mouth the same?
3. What are the products of a healthy tongue?

A Healthy Tongue
Proverbs 21:23; 25:11

Audience: Teenagers

This sermon is going to teach teenagers that not every word should come from your mouth without listening. All the time teenagers must learn to talk only after listening. This is the way you can keep your mouth.

By so doing, it benefits your soul not to get into trouble. Troubles come from the mouth and the tongue. You need to spend your time listening in order that you may create words with knowledge. If you are not keeping your mouth and are not able to control all the words from your mouth, you end up in trouble.

As teenagers, you need to be listening to your parents. Don't talk to your parents and anyone who is bigger than you like you would talk to a child. As you listen, you shall keep your mouth. Remember: your mouth is the source of your life. Keep it diligently, for life is the harvest of a healthy tongue.

Illustration

In our place, we live with monkeys around. During the harvest of crops, monkeys come and eat our crops. During harvest, every farmer searches his fields for monkeys so they won't eat the crops. You know monkeys move in groups. It is easy to hear that monkeys are coming because of the noise from the babies of the monkeys. But there is a monkey which is moving alone. Every farmer is complaining because the monkey eats in the fields without noise. There is no trouble for that monkey like the monkeys who have babies. We learn from this monkey that when you keep your mouth, you benefit without troubles.

Proverbs 21:23   So many times all of us have proven this. Proverbs tell us that wisdom (knowledge of the Bible and how to use it) is greater than might. That is because we talk and then listen.

Proverbs 25:11 indicates that the Word comes in good time, fit to give benefits and health which are the opposite of troubles.

Questions
1. How good is a healthy tongue?
2. How much does it cost you when you keep your mouth?
3. Which type of troubles do you get when you don't keep your mouth?

Living with Integrity
Proverbs 11:27,30; 21:16; 21:21

Solomon advised those who will diligently seek food to seek favor. He simply says: If you are looking for good in your life, the need is not wealth, but the need is favor. Without favor, wealth is in vain.

In Proverbs 11:30, Solomon the son of David says: "The fruit of the righteous is a tree of life." This means that the products of one who learns from wisdom is that he will find a number of good days and have his days multiplied. This is the life of a wise person.

Proverbs 21:16 tells us that whoever strays from the way of understanding shall fall in the company of death. This instructs us to be diligent in understanding. This makes us wise and provides integrity in our life.

In Proverbs 21:21, this verse informs us that to follow righteousness and mercy means we will find life, righteousness and honor. So what? When you hunger and thirst for righteousness, you shall be filled with integrity. When you are in the pipeline of righteousness and mercy, you become an honorable person.

Personal Reflection
As for me, when you want to live a life of integrity you need to take time not to do anything without wisdom. If you don't, what you are doing?

By combining righteousness, mercy, and understanding, you will gain favor. This leads a person to a life of honor with every type of knowledge and health. If you are rich in these areas, no one can blame you, because you become a problem solver with your wisdom.

Finally, when somebody has a lack of knowledge, he or she shall perish. To live without knowledge means you will never enjoy the true life from God, and you will never, ever attempt wisdom.

Illustration

There is a fish called a bream. This fish was always warmer than other types of fish. When this fish found other fish in unity, they were chased by this troubled fish. But one day, a certain man from a nearby village went fishing. As the man reached the dam, he took some small pieces of bread and threw them in the water by the dam.

Fish are tempted when somebody throws something to feed them. Soon after throwing in these small pieces of bread, all the fish came to eat in groups. The bream, who was selfish, was coming to do harm to the other fish. All the fish ran away. The bream started to eat those small pieces. The fisherman put in a hook with a worm. As the bream found the worm, the bream said, "This is a great meal for me!" He took the worm, and the fisherman hooked Bream's mouth. Bream was able to get free. Bream escaped death that day, but the hook left an injury in Bream's mouth until today. That's why bream have a big mouth.

This story teaches us to control our lip. As Proverbs 21:23 says, "Whoever keeps his mouth and his tongue keeps himself out of troubles."

Application

As I reach home my first sermon will be this: Lack of wisdom is the attempt of death. I will also teach different groups based on their needs.

Women: They need to show respect for their husbands and not to be talkative. Instead, they should meditate before they talk.

<u>Adolescents:</u> They must learn from their parents to be aware of the dangers of adultery. The immoral hunters are in their path seeking to snare them during their time of growth. They should not wander far from the teachings of the book of wisdom.

<u>Business owners:</u> They must be wise and show that by what comes from their mouths. From their lips is wealth. They must be able to attend every language because the book of wisdom says that one who live shall live through the fruits of his mouth.

The biggest challenge in my life has been that I have been living like a poor person. I was not aware of the problem. But through the book of Proverbs, I have gained a new hope.

My problem is that I was busy searching for wealth. I was famous as a hard worker but without the success of a worker. It helped when the book of wisdom tells me to first seek favor, and wealth will come.

This book teaches me to know the way that causes favor. I learned through the Bible knowledge that my problem was not my job. But when I got money, I was not asking for wisdom. I spent all my money without removing tithes for God. At the same time, God sent the devourer to eat 10%. As the devourer came, they ate 10% plus 90%. Because I did not separate God's 10%, the other 90% which I needed to save my life was not there. I realized this formation when I heard from the book of wisdom in chapter 1:20-23. Wisdom is calling everywhere.

Terço Florindo

Terço M. Florindo (1975) lives in Chimoio in the country of Mozambique. He has been active in ministry for 13 years and is currently pastoring the local church in Maparanhanga in the Gondola district of Manica province. He has been active in business for 23 years doing everything from stitching shoes to electrical work. Terço's favorite hobbies are reading the Bible and singing worship songs. His favorite verses are Proverbs 1:7, 3:1, 14:5, 17:1, and 27:1. He is married with five children. Terço's advice to young ministers is simple but profound: "Be humble and faithful."

The Source of Wisdom
Proverbs 1:1-7; 22:17-21

Audience: Teenagers

Proverbs 1:2 God gave Solomon the spirit of wisdom. He had the spirit of understanding. He had the spirit of discipline.

Proverbs 1:3 Solomon was the wisest by the grace of God. He was living a righteous life.

Proverbs 1:4 Solomon became wise. He received wisdom from God. He was righteous, and he received the spirit of ruling people.

Proverbs 1:7 When you fear God, it is the beginning of wisdom. The foolish do not accept wisdom. Solomon calls these type of people "the foolish."

Proverbs 22:17 God trains and corrects you to make you better. Your heart must remember the Word of God. Give your ears to hear my words.

Illustration

My personal history: I was raised in the church. My parents were Christians. When I grew, I thought that I was already a Christian because my parents were Christians. In my 14 years, I started to feel and see that I should receive Jesus and be baptized. After receiving baptism, I became a humble young man and obedient from my humility. I felt the wisdom of God in my life, and I took things very seriously. God raised me. Now I am pastoring a church. Everything comes from humility and obedience.

Questions

1. As a young Christian, how can you know that you have wisdom?
2. What do you understand by the word "wisdom"?
3. Does wisdom come from God or from your parents?

Wisdom and Money
Proverbs 3:9-10

Audience: Mixed congregation

Proverbs 10:5 For the rich person, the wealth is his city. The mind of the rich is in his wealth. The wealthy man is the person who has everything in this life.

Proverbs 13:8 The right choice you make reflects your integrity. Obedience brings safety and security.

Proverbs 18:11 The mind of the rich is in his wealth. Don't put your trust in your wealth.

Illustration
In the church that I am leading, there is a man who is rich and always is very worried about his life and wealth. Sometimes he does not come to church because he is taking care of his wealth. In reality, wealth can take a person out of the presence of God. But remember that earthly wealth is the thing of this earth and is not for the kingdom of God. Be careful. Don't put all your trust in wealth because one day it may end.

Questions
1. What do you think of a man who puts his trust in riches?
2. Has wealth ever taken somebody to the kingdom of God?
3. Has wealth come from God in our days?

Personal Reflection
Through scripture, God is teaching me that the rich man is in trouble when he is not fixed in God. For my family, I will teach them that they should not put their trust in their wealth. Then I can help the community by explaining what I have learned during these days.

Wisdom and Money
Proverbs 18:15-17; 28:7

Audience: Mixed congregation

Wisdom comes in two ways: it can be God given, or it can be a result of an energetic search.

Proverbs 18:15-17 The heart of the wise gets knowledge. Be open to new ideas.

Proverbs 28:7 The wise keeps the law in his life. We must keep the command of God in order to have wisdom from God. Be wise and follow the instructions of God.

Illustration
Wisdom is very important in people's lives because when you have wisdom, you will do things in order and in the right time. With wisdom, you can organize the church very well. For me, I thank God for the wisdom that I have. With this wisdom, it makes a church, family and community to progress to another level in their lives. Through His wisdom, I do things in a proper way at the proper time and in a proper order.

Questions
1. What does Solomon mean when he talks about wisdom?
2. What do you understand about wisdom?
3. Is wisdom for everybody or is it only for Christians? Why?

Personal Reflection
Wisdom is the best way in our life, especially as leaders. We need to help people understand things in their lives. I learned that wisdom can be found in a Christian or in an unbeliever. I will teach my family the importance of wisdom. I will even teach the community to transform their ideas and character.

Wisdom and Money
Proverbs 28:6; 19:7; 18:23

Audience: Mixed congregation

The poor fear God and trust in the Lord.
Proverbs 28:6 The poor takes more time in the presence of God in prayer and worship. You can be a poor person in material matters, but in spirit you are rich with God.

Proverbs 19:7 Be sure you understand what you are in the presence of God, not in the presence of man. Follow your friends with spiritual words; don't mind your situation. A poor person is shunned by all his family, but God is in charge.

Proverbs 18:23 The poor asks with a humble heart. It is wrong of the rich to treat the poor with contempt and arrogance. A poor man pleads for mercy.

Illustration
In reality, wisdom and money are things nearly parallel but different. There was a young Christian who had poor wisdom and no money. He was thought of as very poor, and his family and friends abandoned him because he had nothing. But when the wisdom from God began to manifest, he got a business. He had a lot of money accompanied with great wisdom of God. So to be poor is not the end of life, but not having wisdom is almost the end of life.

Questions
1. What do you understand when you hear the word "poor"?
2. Will the poor become rich without wisdom in his life?

Wisdom and Money
Proverbs 11:5-6,10-11

Audience: Mixed congregation

To live in holiness is to live in accordance with the will of God, to have a good relationship with him, and to live life without sin.

Proverbs 11:5-6 God's people are not excluded from problems, but God rescues him or her from trouble. To be wise at home or at church, seek the counsel of others. Righteousness will direct your way and shall deliver you.

Proverbs 11:10-11 When the righteous do well, the city or family prospers. When the righteous get a blessing, the whole city will be blessed. Blessing is for people who live a holy life.

Illustration
When one lives a holy live, God actually blesses him. In the church where I am leading, the youth leader is a young man who fears God and is being blessed. The youth that he is leading are also living lives of blessing. This is happening because in the middle of it is an honest child of God. God raises the saints in their ministries and the cities where they live.

Questions
1. How can you fall when you live as an honest person?
2. Do you believe that the kingdom of God is for saints? Why?
3. Can the city rejoice because of one righteous person?

The Value of Hard Work

Proverbs 6:8-11; 10:4; 14:23; 20:4-13; 24:30-34; 28:19

Commentary

Proverbs 6:8-11 One who works hard hoards his food in the time of harvest. The lazy always is sleeping, crossing his hands. Meanwhile, poverty appears like a thief. Proverbs warns against giving into the temptation of laziness, of sleeping instead of working. We have a weekly day of rest.

Proverbs 10:4 Every day we have time for every opportunity to grow. We can serve and be productive. Yet it is so easy to waste time, letting life slip from our grasp. Refuse to be a lazy person.

Proverbs 14:23 When someone works hard, this always brings great income and advantage. The Bible says in Genesis, "Of your sweat you will eat." When you don't work hard, you will become poor.

Proverbs 20:4-13 If you don't save, you won't have money when you need it. We can't expect God to come to our rescue when we cause our own problem through lack of planning and action. He provides for us, but he also expects us to be responsible. Don't like resting. Open your ideas and views to work hard and have food in your life.

Proverbs 24:30-34 The man without wisdom can't do anything. In his field was a bush, and nothing was there for food. When you live without wisdom, poverty comes with urgency like a thief.

Personal Reflection

It is very important to listen to what wisdom is saying to my personal life. Sometimes God visits me in a vision how to overcome some situation in life. Sometimes some wisdom comes through my family, and we discuss what we can do in that situation. But thank God, because before I make a decision I pray first to have more wisdom.

The biggest challenge is to look upon what my family advises me to do and take that idea and implement it. From now on, I have learned also from the book of Proverbs about wisdom. This teaches me to be serious in my prayers and to focus on the presence of God.

As I learn about wisdom, I will explain to my family how to understand one another and how to respect the ideas of each person using the wisdom of God. In my community, I will encourage them to serve God in order to have good wisdom to overcome satan on some situations or some problem in their lives. In the country, the leaders must ask the presence of God in their ruling before they make a decision.

Alec Jerimani

Alec Jerimani (1977) is the pastor of a local church in Mutari, Zimbabwe. He resides there with his wife and three children. He has been active in ministry for 13 years. Alec also operates a door manufacturing company which has been in operation for 11 years. His favorite hobby is fishing, and his favorite Bible verse is Proverbs 13:4. Alec's advice to young ministers is this: "You reap what you sow."

The Benefits of Wisdom
Proverbs 2:21; 3:13-14; 3:16; 3:23-24

Audience: Mixed congregation

In Proverbs 2:21, wisdom is hereby giving the condition to the congregation that only the upright will benefit in inhabiting the land. Wisdom will benefit the congregation living in truth and also those living with integrity if they remain in it. With wisdom, everything goes as planned and right.

In 3:13-14, if the congregation gains wisdom or if one gets wisdom, he or she is blessed. Since God created the heavens and the earth through wisdom, if you find wisdom you will find the favor of God. Understanding the Word of God is also the benefit of wisdom. Wisdom has more gain than silver, because the benefit of wisdom can't be compared with silver. If you have wisdom, you have the knowledge of God. Wisdom is hereby being explained also to the people that it has more benefits or more profit than gold. God is above all the creation, and all the things and minerals fall under His order.

In verse 3:15, as compared to other things, wisdom is more precious than jewels. There is nothing that you may desire as a congregation which can be compared with God's wisdom.

In 3:16, we are told that if one has wisdom, there is a guarantee of long life in her right hand. There is also riches in her left hand. Wisdom also brings the benefit of honor.

Then in 3:23 the writer explains here to the congregation that if they find wisdom, they are blessed. When they are walking in their ways, they are secured. Their footsteps or feet will not stumble because of wisdom.

Finally, in 3:24 we are told that the one who finds wisdom is blessed because if you lie down you will not be afraid of anything. The writer explains to us that the benefit of wisdom is that even if we are alone and lie down, we are guaranteed of God's presence to keep us. Good sleep is the benefit of wisdom, because in verse 24 it says when you lie down, your sleep will be sweet (God's knowledge).

Illustration

In Proverbs 3:13 it says, "Blessed is the one who finds wisdom and the one who gets understanding." In 2008, I was on duty as a security guard in Zimbabwe at Shakespeare Road, Fairbridge Park. During the night around 0100 hours, armed thieves came to the premises I was guarding. They jumped into the yard. There were three of them. One of them broke into the house. Another one went to the corner. And the third one was waiting at the window so as to receive goods from the one who got inside the house.

I had an idea. I took an empty paper (bag) and put it on my mouth, filled it with pressure and burst it. Then I said with a loud voice of wisdom, "Any movement is a bullet!" They all panicked and remained where they were. I pressed a panic button, and the reaction team came with the police officers and caught the thieves. (Wisdom!) God keeps His people with the benefit of wisdom.

Questions

1. Does it mean people without wisdom won't benefit?
2. Does wisdom have age groups?
3. What can be seen through wisdom?

The Safety of Marriage and Dangers of Adultery

Proverbs 5:1-23; 6:20-35

Audience: Mixed congregation

Proverbs 5:19,20,21,23 In verse 19 Solomon is referring his son to the wisdom of enjoying the blessings through the safety of his own wife, describing her as a lovely deer. His wife will satisfy him and him alone without any danger that may be found through adultery.

In verse 20, his wisdom is warning him against the forbidden woman. To the congregation I remind you that the only safety in life is to be married to your own wife. And avoid hate. In doing so, you will enjoy the safety of marriage.

Verse 21 tells us that man's ways are before God's eyes. If a man is righteous before God, He will bless his life and his marriage, and blessings will follow his life. Marriage is good before God, so He will guide anyone who did it according to his father's instructions.

In verse 23, the safety of marriage in this context is that if a man marries his own wife, he will not die because of lack of discipline and of his great folly. The congregation is being warned of discipline (wisdom).

Illustration

A man shall not live by or with bread alone but by the Word of God. The warning to the young in the congregation is that there are blessings in a good marriage and also there is safety in a good marriage, but also there are very high dangers and risks in adultery. There are several things to be expected after adultery, for example wounds, death and bankruptcy.

Questions

1. Can a man live without adultery?
2. Is marriage good?
3. Is it a blessing to marry?

 WalkwithGod.com Publishing

The Safety of Marriage and Dangers of Adultery

Proverbs 5:1-23; 6:20-35

Audience: Teenagers

In Proverbs 5:17-18, it means that you must have only one wife for yourself and for you alone. You are guaranteed the satisfaction that no one has touched her. The word has put wisdom in you through your choice (rejoice).

In 6:23, if the commandment is a lamp and the teaching is a light and also reproofs bring discipline into the way of life, then teenagers should obey all of them. Through obeying wisdom, they will benefit.

Proverbs 6:25 warns us that the dangers of adultery are that if someone goes into his neighbor's wife, "no one who touches her will be unpunished." There is severe punishment in adultery.

Proverbs 6:32 warns us that it is easy to destroy our life through adultery. The pleasure of sex or adultery will instead bring you wounds and dishonor.

Illustration

In every person's life, there are lusts of the flesh. The flesh and emotions need to be controlled through wisdom. These are blessings in life that you find through your father's wisdom and commandments. Having one good wife is a blessing to your life and your family.

Through adultery, there is no benefit. Instead, your reward is wounds, disappointment, hate, dishonor and all sorts of negative results, if not death. So, teenagers must give their ears to their leaders for the betterment of their future.

Questions
1. Is marriage holy?
2. What are the dangers of adultery?
3. Is wisdom needed in marriage?

Personal Reflection
These scriptures have taught me very important things. God has taught me very much especially in 5:15 to drink water from my own cistern which represents my wife. It is of great importance for a leader to stick to his own wife for the betterment of the church, family, community and town.

God also taught me about the dangers of adultery, which gives bad results of injuries, wounds, and other sorts of dishonor in my life.

When I return back home, I am going to teach my church members about the dangers of adultery and the advantages of teaching children godly things in their homes.

My family is very important to me. I am going to make a timetable to teach them about all the good stuff of Proverbs and wisdom.

In my community, I am going to have a target group of teenagers that I am going to have home groups with so that I will put this knowledge and wisdom to them through teaching them the book of wisdom.

The Safety of Marriage and Dangers of Adultery
Proverbs 5:1-23; 6:20-35

Audience: Teenagers

This sermon is going to talk about Proverbs 5:15-18. In these verses, the father is advising the son to be blessed with his fountain and rejoice in the wife of his youth. In verse 15, he is being advised also to drink water from his own well or cistern, which is the blessing of a wife for him alone. Having his own wife is good, because she will be given to him by God. The son should not forsake Jehovah God, who is responsible for all blessings. Your own wife is a blessing.

When being advised to drink water from your own well, it doesn't mean that there are no other wells. But other wells are not protected and can be poisonous to your health. Giving an example, no one wants his wife to be taken away from him, and the punishment will be big or heavy. Also, there is good satisfaction when you own your own things.

An example from my life is that I married and wedded my beautiful wife. She is a blessing to my life. And I am not forsaken by my father and my God.

Questions
1. What is a blessing?
2. Is having your own wife not a blessing?
3. What is expected of a good son?

The Safety of Marriage and Dangers of Adultery
Proverbs 5:1-23; 6:20-35

Audience: Business Owners

The dangers of adultery in Proverbs 5:10 means you work for others because of adultery. The strangers take their fill of your strength, and your labors go to a stranger's house. Through adultery you have no benefit but loss, because you will be paying for the well (wife) that is not yours.

In verse 11 the results are that your body will be finished or eaten up. You will have no power, and your flesh and body will be consumed. Adultery is not good. It leads you to destruction.

In 6:32, he who commits adultery destroys his life or himself. To business owners, adultery causes their business to go broke because the punishment of adultery is hard. It costs more than it is worth, and there is no benefit in it. Sexual immorality brings diseases and bankruptcy.

In 6:33, the same person who commits adultery will be in danger of getting wounds and dishonor. Also, his disgrace will not be wiped away. Because of dishonor, no one will respect you if you are an adulterer. The dangers will also affect your health, sense and honor.

Questions
1. Is it possible to commit adultery?
2. What is the punishment of adultery?
3. What is meant by water from your own well?

Living with Integrity

Proverbs 3:33-35; 10:22,24,25; 11:30-31; 14:22;
15:26; 17:13; 18:3; 19:29; 21:8,12,16,21; 22:8;
24:8-9; 26:13,27; 28:18; 29:10

Commentary

Proverbs 3:33-35 In these verses, wisdom is teaching you not to be wicked. If you are wicked, the curse of the Lord will come on top of your house. If you are righteous, the blessing will also come to your house. The lesson here is that if you humble yourself before God, His favor is upon your life; but if you are a scorner, He is also scornful of you. You always have to live a life which God will commend as good.

In Proverbs 10:22 the Bible is clearly telling us that the blessing of the Lord is the only thing that makes a person rich. Also, sorrow is not on your side if you are blessed. But to be blessed, integrity is needed in your life.

Proverbs 10:24 tells you that if you do wicked things, you can also expect wicked results in return. But if you desire good things, God will surely grant you righteous things.

The next verse, 10:25, Solomon's proverb in this case is saying if the storm or the problem is no more or passes, no wickedness will find you. The time that it was supposed to take its possession is over. And as for the righteous, he or she is already established and lives forever.

In 11:30, Solomon's proverb is giving a guarantee to you that if you have done a good thing and have done it in a righteous way, you will reap what you sow. Also, you have to be a soul winner, not selfish for your own benefit.

Verse 11:31 tells you that if you are on this earth, you have to fight for righteousness. It has a good benefit in your life. The wicked will also reap what he/she is capable of.

In 14:14, wisdom is telling you that if you do not pour out what is inside yourself, it will just end like a dream. But if you speak it out, sometimes you will enjoy it. If you are good, all the fruits of your ways will be enjoyed.

In 14:22, this proverb tells you that if you do evil things, you have no profit but evil. But in everything good there is celebration, steadfast love and faithfulness.

Verse 15:26 gives you a warning that you shouldn't keep dangerous/wicked things in your mind; one day they will manifest. Those who pour out good things are considered pure before the Lord. Everyone must bear in mind that your words can have profit or loss.

Proverbs 17:13 teaches you to always remember to do good things to those who do bad to you. If you do it the opposite way, you will be addicted to it and will keep it forever.

In 18:3, this verse is telling you through wisdom that bad things call other bad things to happen tomorrow. If you remove honor from your life, you have also removed grace. Keep your honor with you.

Verse 19:29 tells you that there is always a price for what you do. If you do bad things, discipline will be there for you. Also, pain will follow you back if you are a fool. Mend your ways.

In 21:8, you are taught that if you are guilty, you try to act as if you are not guilty. But you can't change it. However, the one who is right will be seen with good conduct.

WalkwithGod.com Publishing

Verse 21:12 encourages you that if you are a person of good behavior or righteous, then keep an eye on the house of the wicked. At last God will bring the wicked to ruin.

In 21:16, you are told that if anyone takes himself from righteous ways and choose the other way, he will get himself the most dangerous end of life.

Verse 21:21is one of the best verses on encouraging you to keep on reading and meditating. Wisdom tells you that if you hunger for good things, you will find righteousness and honor. These are expected of a good Christian.

Proverbs 22:8 is another verse from wisdom. It teaches you that the evil you do is what you have in return — and in a negative way. No excuses.

In verse 24:8 you learn that whatever plan you want to achieve, if it is evil, you will be called a schemer. So as a human being, no one is guaranteed to succeed in evil things. Change your ways.

Verse 24:9 tells you that in living with integrity, it is not advisable to live in sin. Also, by being a scoffer, you are doing an abomination to other people. Whoever mocks someone is recorded as a sinner.

Proverbs 26:1 reminds you that everything has its own season and time. For the one who does not obey the Lord, he will be like that in life.

In 26:3 you are warned that if you do bad things, everyone has his own kind of punishment. There no bad thing worse than the other. Bad is bad; good is good.

Proverbs 26:27 commands you that you should not expect (hope for) bad things to happen to others. If you expect it to your neighbor, it will come to you, because you are the one who wants it. If you start something, it's yours. Face it.

In 28:18, integrity is the key. Wisdom is telling you to be wise. If you don't listen, you will face it or you will fall down.

Finally, in 29:10 wisdom is confirming to you that you must love one another. Do not hate your relative. And the upright fights for his soul or life. Your life is your safe, and your soul is your friend. It must keep you happy always.

WalkwithGod.com Publishing

Stephen Kafula Lunduluka

Stephen Kafula Lunduluka (1968) lives in Lusaka, Zambia where he is planting a new church. He has been active in teaching and prophetic ministry for 29 years. He is married with four children. He has been working as an entrepreneur for five years. His favorite Bible verse is Psalm 23:6. His favorite hobbies include reading books, sharing humor and washing. Stephen's advice to young ministers is: "Ministers should continue following the good example of those who have invested in them by investing in their own lives through evangelism, service and Christian education."

Serving Others
Proverbs 6:12-25; 13:25

Audience: Leaders

A certain pastor of a church was leading his congregation with an iron fist. He used to say, "God cannot speak to any other in this church apart from me," because he was the chosen one and the only official voice of the church. He chose an elder who lived an adulterous life. Just because this elder had money and used to support the pastor's family, he was regarded as a sacred cow which cannot be touched. Because of this attitude by the pastor, the church could not move together with their pastor. This brought about divisions due to the elder's character.

One day a congregant brought a complaint concerning the immoral behavior of the elder who was reportedly visiting the member's wife in the absence of her husband. They had even gone to the extent of having a bath together — with another man's wife! — before the eyes of her children of that family. The children consequently narrated the issue to the father. He also thought it wise to report to the pastor.

The response from the clergyman was negative. He did not show leadership. Instead, he chose to be quiet. When he did address the issue from the pulpit, he said not to touch my anointed one. There was no exposing what was immoral. Equity, justice and truth were not the yardstick. He so much leaned on his own understanding and did not regard others' advice that this led to the downfall of the church. A leader must have a teachable spirit and wisdom for his church to move forward. Poverty and corruption, lies, deception and divisive characters championed this congregation.

Proverbs 6:12-13   A leader must have good morals, a conscience, no deceit and must not be corruptible. When a leader is corrupt, the delivery of goods and services is delayed. Development in a sphere is minimal. Again, there will be nothing to write home about. All in all, the standard of the work of God is truth. The absence of truth will bring about divisions and no direction. Because each one is living for himself, the unity of purpose will be not achieved.

Proverbs 13:25   The scripture is emphasizing that using righteousness from the light of the Word of God will make us content. Our own righteousness is like filthy rags. It's the same as saying we are laboring in vain. Success comes from a righteous attitude, a righteous conduct, and a righteous implementation. The results will be tangible. The wicked will yearn but will not eat the fruit of righteousness. The principle of sowing and reaping applies here.

Proverbs 29:7 A leader's main purpose is to lift the standard of his followers. The leader must care for anyone regardless of his or her status in society. The "love all, serve all" principal must be applied.

Proverbs 30:25 The ants are very small but extremely wise. The ants have a unity of purpose, one aim, teamwork and good communication which consequently produce good results. They are a people that know the seasons, and they believe in themselves.

Proverbs 18:20,21 A leader must have a vision. This vision must be spelled out to the followers so that from the fruit of his mouth, the stomach will be filled. If a roadmap is put in place, the benchmarks will tell us where we are going. This will result in achieving our goal. Negative pronouncers will not bring the desired progress. A positive attitude and a mission statement will bring deliverance to the people.

Living Righteously

Proverbs 12:2-5; 13:9,21,25; 11:5-6

Audience: Mentors and leaders

Questions
1. What is a mentor or leader?
2. What is a spiritual mentor?
3. What are the greatest benefits that would come from a mentor?

A mentor or leader is a pilot, engineer, or a compass that gives direction. The community cannot live righteously without a mentor. A leader must be a product of some discipline, which means he/she must be trained and disciplined by others and go out to live by example.

The community we live in is characterized by abuse of alcohol, child marriages, prostitution, poverty, etc. These elements have affected our society badly, and sanity must come in to rescue the society from the things listed above. A mentor can be a teacher, pastor, parent or social worker who can help to differentiate right from wrong. A mentor must be principled, rooted in the art of correction or counseling. Living righteously can only come about when people who are leaders start teaching the society what can bring about a perfect society free from the vices pointed out.

The righteous in the community are like a light which shines and consequently gives direction. Then righteousness protects the community. Information is power, and living righteously is displayed when you fight poverty which illiteracy brings about, help to establish recreation centers for youths, provide training opportunities for all ages, distribute information on everyone's level of consumption, and engage in regular mentoring. Such edification will bring about a response from the community. A mentor must lead by example, be a facilitator of healthy habits, and show wisdom in day to day deliberations.

A spiritual mentor is almost the same as a regular mentor, except that the point of view is different. A man who is born in a sinful nature is bound to error; thus, there is the need to bring in the spiritual aspect. Without wisdom as the first thing, all that we see around us could not be there. Wisdom must take its course, because she has everything.

Mentors need wisdom desperately for them to deliver the goods and services. This leads to living righteously. We can talk about an honest society, but talking alone won't suffice. We need to put up benchmarks to tell whether we are on course or not. Wisdom must come in to do a perfect job.

If he does his homework properly and sticks to the rules of the game, the greatest benefits that would come from a mentor are: we will have no child marriages, poverty will be eradicated through education, abuse and alcohol and drugs will be a thing of the past, notorious gangs of robbers will be eradicated. The behavior of our community will be good, and consequently we will be living righteously.

Illustration
A street kid turns out to be a pastor. Luke is born in a family of 6 children, 3 girls and 3 boys. He is the second born in the family. His parents are still alive but not in gainful employment. For this family to be fed was very challenging because of the situation of the boy's parents. Luke had friends who he was found with most of the time. They came up with the idea of going to beg for some money and food on the streets in town. The boy was so much in the act that he decided to live in the streets with his colleagues. Life in the street is about stealing, drug abuse, sexual immorality, drunkenness, and not going to school. One day, a group of Christian believers were on an outreach mission. They befriended Luke and his friends. They

started talking to them about Jesus, about their lives and about the benefits they can get once they accept Jesus as their Savior. They trusted the team, did exactly what they asked, and were born again. Luke started an outreach program to the same people he came from, and because his friends knew him, they started following him.

Steps in the Right Direction
Proverbs 14:11,19,34; 21:19

Questions
1. When you were a child, did you ever have a scary moment like when the lights were turned off in the room at night and you couldn't see your way out?
2. When we lose our foothold in life, it can be a scary thing. How does the Word of God help us keep our foothold?

In this lesson, we are focused on how God brought David out of the pit. In this lesson, we are focusing on the latter part of the verse which says righteousness makes a nation to stand, and sin disgraces the nation.

A renewed foothold: When a nation has neglected the godly course, it will not stand. The builders whom Jesus talked about in the Gospels were about building a family on a sure foundation. By wisdom, houses are built and finished. In the absence of it, destruction will definitely visit the house, and it will not stand.

1. Realization: For us to be guided in the right direction, repentance must be done. This is the total about face of events and life.
2. Acceptance: After repenting, admittance must be achieved for the Savior of the Word of God to come in to rescue us.
3. Sensitization also must play a major role in the process of taking steps in the right direction. Counseling is very costly and will need a lot of effort to achieve the intended purpose.
4. Follow up is also another aspect that must be embraced for us to achieve the goal.

Getting Wisdom
Proverbs 9:7-9

Getting wisdom is a matter of choice. Some want it while the other group is not interested. Correcting or advising a fool is a waste of time. It's like sowing seeds on a concrete floor.

Correction and discipline in life are vital for one to achieve his/her goal. If somebody is prideful and thinks he knows it all, even if you use the most refined words, he/she won't appreciate them because he/she is puffed up with false knowledge. In other words, it doesn't pay to correct a proud son, because he won't appreciate it. But if you spend your time correcting a simple man, he will love you and appreciate it and consequently a very strong bond will develop between mentor and student.

Questions
1. Who is a conceited man?
2. How can a man with pride be helped?
3. Is there any conscience in a conceited man?
4. Why is it that a conceited man is offended when he is corrected, but on the other hand when the simple man is corrected, he accepts and works on his mistakes?

Our parents know us and understand us better than anyone. They know even which child to trust with wisdom and leadership. A wise parent will invest his time, money, and effort on the ground which he is sure will reward him/her in some way. Some children hate correction. It's always them who want to carry the day when it comes to correction. A foolish child makes his/her parents to walk with their head bowed down due to shame. The simple child gets counsel from his parents. By so doing, this is an honor to the parents. It will make them walk with a lifted head in the streets of their community.

Parents, Help Your Children Get Wisdom

Proverbs 3:1-2

Here in these verses, the Holy Spirit is emphasizing not forgetting the teachings of wisdom. You cannot do without wisdom. Prosperity and long life all lie in the teaching of wisdom. Success in life comes by way of understanding and by acquiring knowledge and wisdom.

Wisdom is the focal point. Wisdom is saying to my life to not forget the advice from wisdom. Treasure it always. Use wisdom all the time. Apply it in all life situations, and success is guaranteed.

Questions

1. Why is the father encouraging the son not to forget and always remember what he has told him to do?
2. What does the father want to see in his son's life?
3. What is expected always from the son?
4. If the son wants to see a long and prosperous life, what must he do?

For the Parents

The writer is encouraging parents to spend quality time with their children. During this same period, the parents who are the child's primary source of wisdom can now instruct, teach, correct, and edify the child in the way he/she should go. Every well-meaning parent wants a good report from their children, but this can only come about when somebody is well informed by his parents.

Giving and Accepting Counsel

Proverbs 3:1-2; 9:7-9; 11:14; 12:15

Audience: Leaders

Our society today lacks leaders. Skills, credentials and titles are not rare, but leaders are very scarce. A leader must know that the Church is like Noah's ark which accommodated all kinds of animals: the biggest and the smallest, the fastest and the slowest. For every society to prosper, the unity of purpose must be realized, and the stakeholders' (followers) contributions must be highly regarded.

A leader is a pilot, an engineer, a pioneer, which means he must have a roadmap spelled out. It must be clear, and the society he is leading must benefit at the end of the day. The leader must accommodate each and every member regardless of his status.

A follower's contribution is vital, accepting and giving advice or counsel as required. Some leaders find it difficult to accept advice or counsel. They want to give advice to their followers all the time. They do not want to be corrected. Instead, they refer to credentials, and their own opinion is the best. If a leader is not accommodating his followers, he/she will consequentially become a lone ranger. The group will therefore be torn apart. Once they divide themselves, the unity of purpose is defeated, and this will bring about the downfall.

A good leader can succeed when he chooses to listen to his followers' opinions. He must just facilitate. The followers must play a major role. The followers' contributions must be treasured, taken so that the people can own the intended project.

The scripture clearly states that the way of a fool seems right to himself, but the wise listen to advice. In a multitude of counselors, the king is sure, and security is guaranteed. Good leadership must have a listening ear and a discerning heart. Moses tried to play it all by himself, but his father-in-law (who was possibly an idol worshipper) saw a problem in what his son-in-law was doing to the people and himself. He counseled Moses and told him what was best for him and the people.

Because wisdom is humility, the son-in-law took his advice. There was specialization, and division of labor carried the day. Efficiency was realized, and it's still working today. A leader must know that in his/her followers, there is a lot of potential which must be utilized to the benefit of the society. The leader must be friendly and must learn to take sense out of nonsense. He must implement the ideas and then evaluate critically to learn from the mistakes made in the past.

Accepting and giving advice is a major component for any society to prosper. No group can succeed without this important aspect of wisdom. Wisdom is the focal thing. Without it, nothing can be achieved.

Proverbs 3:1-2 The mission of all of us since the fall of the earth is to succeed or to prosper. That's why in this passage we find the father advising the son to not forget the teachings he got from him. He is encouraging him to remember them, live by them, and keep them in the heart, so that his mission of prosperity may be possible and the days of his life prolonged. King Solomon knew what was good for his son. That is why he emphasized to keep the commands. This means the son was left with no other wise choice but to do what his father asked him to do.

Proverbs 9:7-9 Some people are so stubborn that they cannot be corrected. Advising them will be like insulting them. They feel they know it all, so correcting them will be like insulting them. There are also people who want to learn. They love correction. Wisdom is about ever learning, and there's no end to it. If you want to be wise, accept advice. And ask where you have failed if you are not clear.

Proverbs 10:8 The wise in the heart will always treasure advice, while the folly will turn down every good intention. The wise is always focused and very much interested in the future, but the fool is always thinking about today. And because of this different point of view, the fool will come to ruin while, on the other hand, the wise will prosper.

Sydney Kapungwe

Sydney Kapungwe is the senior pastor of Philadelphia Church of God in Lusaka, Zambia. He also serves as the District Overseer for Central Zambia and is the Acting National Youth Director. He is married to Jacqueline Sande with whom he has four children. He also runs a construction company, Herpenden Investment, Ltd. His hobby is hunting. His favorite Bible verse is Romans 8:1. His advice to younger ministers is: "Prepare yourselves for service to equip the Church for spiritual insight and godly leadership."

The Rewards of Following God
Proverbs 3:25-26; 29:6; 8:32-36

Audience: Mixed congregation

Proverbs 3:25-26 states that when you heed the instructions from God, you should not be afraid of any terror or wicked thing when it comes upon your life. God will be able to rescue you from harm. Be confident with God. He will prevail and protect you from falling. When you wholeheartedly follow the steps of the Lord, your enemies shall not be able to catch you.

In 29:6, the evil man is caught in his sins, but whoever follow the Lord will blessed. And the blessing of God does not add any sorrow. Whoever follows God is rewarded abundantly. He/she will sing and praise God for following God.

In chapter 8, there is a reward for whoever follows the Lord. This reward is the benefit of following the instructions given by God. Proverbs 8:32 states that whoever listens to God is blessed. Rewards come from God to repay only those who listen and obey God's words. The Bible states, "the truth shall set you free." Whenever you decide to follow God's instruction or truth, you shall receive the reward.

In Proverbs 8:35, this verse clearly indicates that whoever finds the truth, finds life. I am an example. Had I not been following God, I would have gone astray or died a long time ago. Most of my childhood friends who did not follow God have either died or are in the world enjoying the desires of the flesh which produce death or a curse. As the Bible says again in 8:36, whoever fails to find the truth brings injury on himself. All who hate wisdom, love death.

In Proverbs 1:23-28, the scripture states that whoever refuses the counsel of God, calamity will come upon him. God is always

 WalkwithGod.com Publishing

calling every person to repent or come to Him, but we usually ignore His calling and hence receive the consequence which is not favorable. Eventually, we lose our precious lives. In verse 28, God reminds us that wisdom does not listen to whoever refuses instruction even when he calls for help when calamity or terror comes upon him. This is simply because he hates knowledge. God's counsel makes people receive His blessing and safety. The counsel of God builds good character in people's lives.

Questions
1. What makes people not follow God?
2. Do your decisions determine your future?
3. What is your choice in your life?

Family Relationships: A Wise Son

Proverbs 1:8-9; 10:1; 15:20

Audience: Congregation

Proverbs 1:8-9   In verse 8, the Bible states that it's imperative for the son to hear from the parents' instruction so as to avoid falling into an unwise path. Blessing comes from observing instruction from both the father and the mother.

In 10:1 it states that the wise son is a delight to his father because he listens to the instruction and obeys the advice of the father. The son who does not listen to instruction is a source of sorrow to the mother. A wise son makes the parents glad.

Proverbs 15:20 also refers to the wise son as a blessing to the father. When a son is able to observe and walk in the counsel of the parents (both the father and the mother), he is really a blessing. He makes the father proud and glad, and he is not a disgrace to the mother.

Illustration

Young men mostly fall into worldly pleasures because of failing to observe instructions from the parents or guardians. I have my nephew who decided to go his own way despite several advices against his lifestyle which was ungodly. He ended up involved in criminal activities, and currently he is in police custody because of unwise decisions. Young men should be a good example and live a meaningful life that pleases God and parents. Unwise behavior could ruin their lives.

Family Relationships: A Foolish Son

Proverbs 19:13,26; 17:25

Proverbs 19:13 tells us that a disgraced son is a pain to his father. A foolish son always brings shame to his father, and he does not live a blessed life. He does not live as expected. As the Bible states, you must honor your parent for you to live long.

In 19:26, the behavior of the son chases the parents. The bad character of the son brings shame to the father and the mother. And he usually brings violence to the parent. Such a son is a total disgrace.

Proverbs 17:25 reminds us that it's only the foolish son who brings grief to the father because of his wrongdoing. That does not please the father. He also brings pain and misery to his mother.

Foolish sons usually end up in misery and in a disgraceful lifestyle because of the distance they create between themselves and their parents. They end up in jail, and some die an untimely death because they bring grief to the father and mother. Because of not observing counsel from their parents, they become vulnerable, street kids, criminals, and such things.

Family Relationships: A Good Wife

Proverbs 12:4; 14:1; 18:22; 19:14

Proverbs 12:4 states that an excellent wife is the crown of her husband. Every good wife makes the husband or house stable. The husband is respected, and he cherishes her in her good conduct. But the wife who does not abide in the counsel of the husband is a shame to him.

Proverbs 14:1 tells us that the good and wise wife builds her house. The seasoned woman always makes a stable house because she understands the needs of a good home.

Proverbs 18:22 says that it's from a good wife where favor is enjoyed. A good wife indeed comes from God, and whoever finds her obtains success.

Proverbs 19:14 reminds us that all of the world's riches are inheritable, but a good wife comes from the Lord. Finding a good and prudent wife is a blessing from the Lord. Godly women are rare to find.

Good wives build their houses, and they are a blessing to their husbands. When the house is brought into order by the prudent wife, we see success and joy. I have observed homes run by good wives. The children are usually a good moral example for the rest of the other families. I was brought up by a godly mother who always guided me when I was a teenager, and I decided to follow the steps of my godly mother.

In short, a good wife helps the family to become godly, and she is a blessing to the husband and the entire family.

Family Relationships: A Quarrelsome Wife

Proverbs 21:9; 25:24; 27:15

Audience: Women

Proverbs 21:9 tells us that it's not easy to live in a house with a quarrelsome wife. It's better to live somewhere else where there's peace. A quarrelsome wife disturbs the peace of the house. Usually the husband prefers to live alone rather than with such a wife.

In 25:24, the safest place to live is a place of calmness than to have a quarrel with a wife. The quarrelsome wife makes the house unstable. She does not value marriage. Hence, she disturbs her husband with hateful words.

Then in 27:15, it states that the dripping of rain in the house is like a woman who is quarrelsome. A troublesome wife brings constant uneasiness in the husband's life. The house is likely to experience constant problems with such a quarrelsome wife.

Illustration

Marriages are usually destroyed because of quarrelsome wives who usually do not accept their behavior. Divorce seems like a solution to some of the husbands who do not think like a Christian or who cannot continue living in the environment of noise and pain. The character of such a wife brings about separation and hate to both her husband and her children. She is not a good example to the other women who need her counsel. The quarrelsome wife provokes her husband by her words which often disturbs the peace in their marriage.

The Value of Hard Work
Proverbs 6:9-11; 10:4,26; 12:24,27; 13:4; 14:23;15:19; 16:26; 18:9; 19:15,24; 20:4,13; 21:17; 24:30-34; 26:14-15; 28:19

Commentary

Proverbs 6:9-11 states whoever loves sleeping rather than working, such a person will also use excuses to avoid work. He will continue appealing to sleep saying, "I have to sleep a little. I have no time for work." Poverty will come to such a person who does not love to work. Prosperity or money is earned through hard work by using one's own hands. Whoever does not work does not receive money. It is a warning to such a person who is lazy and loves sleeping because it only leads to poverty and suffering.

Proverbs 10:4 states that whoever is idle, careless or inactive and neglects work through lazy behavior will lose a job opportunity. But a person who does the work diligently will have plenty and earn much.

Proverbs 12:24,27 state that those who are diligent and faithful are able to have wealth and power to rule, but the slothful or deceitful shall earn nothing.

Proverbs 13:4 states that he shall be enriched with the fruit of his own labor. Working hard brings payment as a result of diligently moving towards achieving the desire of your heart. Hence, you will eat the fruit of your labor.

Proverbs 14:23 teaches us that the richness in life is found through hard work and extra work. Every labor gains a good result of profit, but talking does not produce anything. Every achievement is associated with hard work. Laboring and toiling produce much progress. It may be tough and tiresome to do work, but it pays off at the end of the work.

Proverbs 15:19 states that because of being a sluggard, life will be full of complications and difficulties which he cannot manage to pass through. It becomes hard to live or to do business. For the sluggard, life becomes discouraging and not conducive. But to the honest or upright, life is a blessing because of the element of honesty, integrity and truthfulness.

Proverbs 16:26 states that it's through labor that food is prepared. Whoever does not want to work, let him not eat. The condition for enjoying your life is labor or work without which suffering and poverty come.

Proverbs 18:9 A wasteful person does not enjoy his life. It's his act of negligence to his work which brings pain and suffering to his own life.

Proverbs 19:15,24 state that the lazy person is always too tired to do the work. Because of his habit, he becomes poor and has no food to prepare for himself. He is dangerous to his health and family. Lack of work brings nothingness and hunger. The sluggard would rather starve than take pains to feed himself. He will not take his hand out of his bosom to take food out of the dish to feed himself.

Proverbs 20:4 tells us that during plowing, the sluggard decides to avoid cultivating. This means that the sluggard, under the pretense of bad weather, neglects cultivating his own land till the plowing period is elapsed. Every season has its purpose, and missing opportunity in life is miserable.

Proverbs 20:13 states that as much as sleep is natural and a gift from God, everything has its opportunity, including sleep and awakening. Too much sleep hinders progress. There should be time to do work rather than love sleeping which leads to hunger.

Proverbs 21:17 states that love of pleasures leads to poverty. A careless lifestyle really does not promote hard work, and usually it only brings hunger. Someone who loves pleasure does not cherish hard work but only things that come through wishing. Most people who love pleasure are lazy, and they suffer poverty and anguish.

Proverbs 24:30-34 states there are things that seem right in a man's eyes, but it leads to nothing. And in these verses, the writer has an insight into the life of a lazy person who carelessly lives a worthless life and yet does not see this as abnormal. His life is full of filthy things, bad character, moral compromise, a broken life. He enjoys it. But the wise person sees differently and acknowledges his way of living. These verses also acknowledge that love of more sleep eventually leads to poverty. Usually, laziness is like a trap of hunger and poverty. It strikes unknowingly.

Proverbs 28:19 Although preparing the land becomes hard and boring, it produces plenty of harvest which provides food to the family as well as to the community. Meanwhile, others who decided to do other things are mostly coming to poverty. Farming requires hard work during its season, but harvest time produces enough food which benefits the one who labors. There could not be wealth or prosperity without tilling of the land for cultivation.

Personal Reflection

The scriptures from the book of Proverbs not only encourage me to work hard but also remind me that laziness and personal philosophy can lead people to extreme poverty and anguish for the rest of their lives.

God is reminding me to do whatever I want to do in life with diligence, that Christianity is not only a personal relationship with God but a commitment to work with my hands so as to provide food for my family. Hard work produces progress which does not bring regrets in one's life. The blessing of the

Lord does not add any sorrow. The scripture from Thessalonians says "Whoever does not want to work, let him not eat." It's through work that we live or sustain life while mere words or arguments produce nothing.

You cannot achieve anything without planning. Lack of planning has been a challenge to some of the work which I usually want to start. Another challenge is motivation from the family and a lack of resources to invest in the business. Other challenges including sickness, climate change, and a lack of risk taking have been taking me to an unproductive situation which eventually leads me to regret or poverty.

There are some perspectives that seem productive yet which do not produce any positive results. That really is where God has been reminding me to change for the sake of progress. I need to change bad company for people who are good and noble friends, and I need to commit every work into His hands.

It has not been difficult to obey God's advices because of what I have been going through in life. That has taught me to always commit every program to God. Recently I have been adamant to obey God's words that lead me in spite of failure.

I believe I will overcome through the changing of my perspective towards God's counsel through committing every one of my plans in a word of prayer. By accepting my flaws, it has been the turning point. Without several words of advice, plans are hindered. I have been listening to advice and also learning from past experience, and this has helped to build a new chapter in my life.

The value of hard work is to have the spirit of teamwork. This cannot be achieved without the involvement of others. For a business to grow, there is need for consultation and research of that particular line of business. No church growth comes without the formation of leaders and also delegation. Personal discipline is paramount to hard work and progress. Consistence is also important: always maintain your plans and concepts, because sometimes results take a long time to come.

Hard work has produced much results in the establishment of the local church. It took patience and consistency to have a church with two families meeting in my house grow to a membership of one hundred. Tjrough visitation and prayer meetings, other people were mobilized to be a part of the vision.

We drew a plan through which several activities were to be done, and we worked with them. That included the necessary requirements to open a branch (church plant): instruments, chairs, church programs. We worked on this tirelessly, and eventually the church was opened. A month later we had 80 members. The value of working hard produces the desires of your hearts.

Afonso Mabucuro

Afonso Franisse Mabucuro (1966) serves as the pastor of Ferroviário Church of God in Maputo in the country of Mozambique. He also serves as the National Secretary of Church of God World Missions in Mozambique. Afonso has been in ministry for 14 years and has also been active in a driving school business for 11 years. He is married with five children. His favorite verses are Proverbs 23:15,19, 20,22 and 23. The advice he offers to young ministers is, "My son, if your heart is wise, let my heart also rejoice. Hear, O my son, and be wise, and straighten thine heart in the way. Do not be with wine drinkers or meat eaters. Hearken to your father who begot you, and when your mother grows old, do not despise her. Buy the truth, and do not sell it, wisdom, instruction, and insight."

The Virtuous Woman
Proverbs 31:10-31

Audience: Women

Proverbs 31:10 The most important woman is a woman of noble character. A woman may live in the world but not have a good life because her character is not noble.   In our church and community, we need women whose character is more valuable than rubies.

Proverbs 31:11 Confidence is very important in a couple. In this verse we see and we read that the husband has full confidence in his wife. In her home or her family, she makes all things in order, and this helps her husband.

Proverbs 31:15 The virtuous woman gets up while it is still dark to prepare all things for her family (her husband and children). She provides food for her family. She has portions for her servant girls to do work in the home.

Proverbs 31:23 Her husband is respected at the city gate because the way his wife lives adds to his honor. He takes his seat among his community; this is a place of respect. The man who has a virtuous wife will respect her in the land and community where he lives.

Proverbs 31:26-28 She speaks with wisdom. This means that the woman who knows God teaches and gives the faithful instruction which is on her tongue. Her whole family respects her, and the community knows that she is a good example.

Proverbs 31:30 The woman who puts her charm first is deceptive. This woman does not exercise wisdom to help her family. She thinks in her heart that she is beautiful, but this is fleeting. The most important thing is to do something to help the family and community where we live. Whoever fears the Lord is to be praised. God gives such a woman His wisdom.

Illustration

Here is a story to illustrate the woman of noble character. Some people have the mistaken idea that the ideal woman in the Bible is retiring, servile and entirely domestic. Not so. This woman is an excellent wife and mother. She is also a manufacturer, importer, manager, realtor, farmer, and seamstress. Her strength and dignity do not come from her amazing achievements, however. They are a result of her reverence to God.

In our society where physical appearance counts for so much, it may surprise us to realize that her appearance is never mentioned.   Her attractiveness comes entirely from her character. The woman described in Proverbs has more abilities than the woman who puts her family's social position high.

Perhaps we can't be just like her in the same details, but we can learn from her industry, integrity, resourcefulness, encouragement, care for others, and her concern for the poor. These qualities, when coupled with fearing God, show us how to become wise, make good decisions, and live according to God's ideal. Thank you and God bless you all. Amen.

Questions

1. Where can you find a woman of noble character?
2. What is important in a virtuous woman?
3. How can the man or husband put confidence in his wife?

Giving Control to God
Proverbs 10:27; 14:26-27; 28:26; 29:25

Audience: Children under 12

Proverbs 10:27 I would like to teach the children to know God. He is the Lord who gives life. It is necessary to have the fear of the Lord because it adds length of life. The years of the wicked are cut short. You, children, are now very young, and you would like to have a long life. You need to know God and fear Him. He will give good and long life in this world.

Proverbs 14:26-27 These verses demonstrate that the fear of the Lord is a fountain of life, turning a man away from the snares of death. The one who fears the Lord has a secure fortress. His children will be in a place of refuge. My friends, if you would like to have success in your life, fear God. He will give you a long life and good health in the world.

Proverbs 28:26 We see in this verse that the one who trusts in himself is a fool. But he who walks in wisdom is kept safe. My sons and daughters, take wisdom from the Lord and walk in it. You will be safe. The wise person depends on God.

Proverbs 29:25 In this verse we learn that those who fear people can be hampered in everything they try to do. In an extreme form, it can make you afraid to leave your home. By contrast, fear of God (respect, reverence, and trust) is liberating. It's God who can turn the harm intended by others into good for those who fear Him and trust Him.

Questions
1. Should you fear people who cannot do eternal harm to you?
2. Do you like long life?
3. Why does the wise person depend on God?

Giving Control to God

Proverbs 14:2,12,25-27; 16:9,25; 19:3; 26:12; 27:1; 28:14

Audience: Men

The Wisdom to Choose the Way
Proverbs 14:2,12,25-27; 16:9,25 I look forward to teaching the men of my local church when I return home. It is very important to inform them about wisdom and how they can walk in this world. Each of them are men whose calling is to serve God. The man who walks uprightly shows that he fears the Lord. It is important to help men to understand that God sees all thing. His eyes do not sleep.

Proverbs 19:3 We men sometimes are tempted to walk in our own folly. If we do, our life comes to ruin. But in our heart, we are angry against the Lord. We say, "God does not love me" and "Where is the Lord to help to save my life?" We forget that we practiced folly and did not use wisdom from the Lord. That is because we did not ask Him to give us wisdom to walk in the light of God.

Proverbs 26:12 This verse teaches men to be humble. If you are wise in your own eyes, there is more hope for a fool than for you. This is because you are depending on your knowledge. Instead, ask God for wisdom, and give Him your way or life. He will turn your life around to good health.

Proverbs 27:1 In this verse we learn not to boast about tomorrow. We do not know what a day may bring forth. It teaches us that we can plan all that we can for tomorrow, but it is important to deposit our plan with God. He will give us each day to do what we need to do.

Proverbs 28:14 Finally, in this verse we can see that a blessing is upon the man who always fears the Lord. All your ways will be blessed, and everything will go well. But whoever hardens his heart falls into trouble.

All of you brothers, give me your hearing today. Fear the Lord. Give Him your way, your life, your family, and you see that you will begin to receive blessing from God.

Illustration

The story is based in Proverbs 27:1. This is a true word. We cannot boast about tomorrow, for we do not know what a day may bring forth. The word in Isaiah 5:2 demonstrates that when we make a plan, it is necessary to ask God about it and place our faith in Him. The man in Isaiah dug up the ground, cleared it of stones and planted it with the choicest vines. He then built a watchtower in it and cut out a winepress as well. But when he looked for a crop of good grapes, he found that it yielded only bad fruit. This man was hoping to receive good fruit, but he did not. We need to pray and realize that God is in control, because scripture has said, "Don't worry about what you will eat, because the Lord will provide for you."

Questions

1. Why does the man who hardens his heart fall into trouble?
2. What do you think this means when it says that a man plans his course in his heart, but the Lord determines his steps (Proverbs 16:9)? Why?
3. Do you know a wise man?

Giving Control to God
Proverbs 15:3,33; 16:1,33; 19:21; 20:24

Audience: Women

Fear God
Proverbs 15:3,33 Using this verse, I would like to teach the women to know that God is in all places and that He sees what we think and do. Know that the eyes of the Lord are everywhere keeping watch on the wicked and the good. He sees both the evil actions and the evil intentions lying behind them. He is not an indifferent observer. One day He will wipe out evil and punish the evildoers, just as He will establish the good and reward those who do His will.

I would like to invite all women to know the fear of the Lord which teaches a human being wisdom and humility. When a woman seeks wisdom from God, she will become a woman of noble character and will be respected by her family, husband, children and community.

Proverbs 16:1,33 Women, like everyone else, use their lips to talk. In this verse, I want to teach you that God gives the ultimate answer (reply of the tongue). Remember that in spite of all our efforts, God is ultimately in control. He wants us to use our minds, to seek the advice of others, and to plan. Nevertheless, the results are up to Him. All woman should live for Him. Ask for guidance as you plan, and then act on your plan as you trust in Him.

Proverbs 20:24 Finally, in this verse we are told that our steps are directed by the Lord. Because of this, there is not anyone who can fully understand his own ways. This verse counsels us not to worry if we don't understand everything as it happens. Instead, we should trust that God knows what He's doing, even if His timing or decision is not clear to us. But we have the promise of God's direction in our life. This is the one and very important truth for women to remember.

Illustration

I recall a problem that happened last year, where a conflict arose caused by the local church pastor of Matola. She also led the Women's Ministry of Maputo Province. This pastor created a group of intercessors. During the prayer sessions, they began to prophesy and use black magic to command demon spirits and make them speak. However, using black magic is not biblical.

Some members of the local church council in Matola denounced these practices, because the spirits or demons should only be expelled with the power of the Holy Spirit. Since God watches everything, He denounced the existence of these heretical doctrines which are not teachings of the Church of God.

During one prayer session, because the demonic spirits showed resistance to leave, the shepherdess (lady pastor) instructed some of the ladies to strip off their clothing in order to scare away the demons and to cure the sickness. The Bishop of the Church in Mozambique has disciplined this pastor and removed her from her leadership position.

In conclusion, I want to call attention to holiness, because God sees everything done in secret. You can do nothing hidden. It will all come out. God is faithful, and the eyes of God see everywhere. I encourage all you sisters to fear God, doing well in works, evangelism and demonstrating the way and the light from God. Blessings.

Questions

1. Who makes sure that plans will happen?
2. Why does the Lord come and give the reply of your tongue?
3. How then can anyone understand his own way?

Giving Control to God

Proverbs 3:5-8; 16:3-4,20; 18:10; 19:23; 21:22,30-31

Audience: Mixed congregation

Proverbs 3:5-8 These verses discuss about giving control to God. The one who trusts in the Lord with all his heart does not lean on his own understanding. If the congregation acknowledges God in their ways, He will make their paths straight. All members must not be wise in their own eyes. It is necessary to fear the Lord because it will bring health to your body and nourishment to your bones.

Proverbs 16:3-4,20 In your lives, commit to the Lord whatever you do, and all your plans will succeed. God is not like all the proud of heart. Be sure of this: He will not punish them. When we are in the church, we come to God to deposit our hearts and minds to Him.

Proverbs 18:10 In this verse we see that the name of the Lord is a very strong tower. The righteous run to His name and are safe. Can you tell me, brothers and sisters, who does not like to be safe? I think all the congregation wants to have a good life!

Proverbs 19:23 In this verse, we learn that our fear of the Lord leads to life contentment, untouched by trouble. Who of you in this church does not rest content and is not free from trouble? This verse is for you.

Proverbs 21:22,30-31 In these verses, we will learn that a wise man attacks the city of the mighty and pulls down the stronghold in which they trust. In God, there is no wisdom or plan that can succeed against the Lord. The last verses say that you can prepare for the day of battle, but victory rests with the Lord. Can you tell me who does not like victory over his enemy? I think that everyone likes victory, and in this sermon, we discover where the solution is. Come to the Lord, not to me, your Pastor. The Lord will gain the victory.

Proverbs 22:12 Finally, in this verse, we learn that God keeps watch over knowledge, but He frustrates the words of the unfaithful. Tell me, my brothers and sisters, who does not like the eyes of the Lord to keep watch over him? When you want to, deposit your heart and your knowledge in God. God bless all. Amen.

Questions
1. What will happen to people who love God?
2. God protects and rewards those who make the commitment to follow Him. Is this affirmation true?
3. Can you use your own words to explain this to others?

Lessons for Godly Leadership

Proverbs 15:22; 16:10,12-15; 19:12; 20:8,28;
22:11; 24:21-22; 29:4,14

Commentary

Proverbs 13:17 In this verse we understand that the pastor or leader who is a wicked messenger will fall into trouble. His pastoring or his leadership will not be successful. But the leader or pastor who comes from God brings with him healing for the people of God.

Proverbs 14:28,35 In verse 28, we understand that the pastor who does not have members in his church is ruined. We are leaders when we have a congregation to lead, and when we have a large population, we are leaders. Verse 35 teaches me that in our church, we need to be wise servants in order to take forward the gospel and all the jobs we do in the church.

Proverbs 15:22 This verse teaches us that when we make a plan, we will become successful when seek more counsel. This give us many good opinions for godly leadership of the church. When we do not go to people who can advise us, the plan fails. We need the help of those who can enlarge our vision and broaden our perspective.

Proverbs 16:10,12-15 These verses teach that a good leader keeps in his lips an oracle, but his mouth should not betray justice. It is good for everyone who is a leader of the people or community or church to do this. Justice is fundamental to leadership. True and honest lips bring pleasure. A leader will value someone who speaks like that. The wise man will appease the wrath of the leader. Whenever the king's face or the leader's face brightens, it means life. It is compared to a rain cloud in spring.

Proverbs 17:7,11 These two verses are very important for me. When we accept Jesus Christ, then He is our only Savior. We need the pastor or leader of a church to not be arrogant, because that cannot bring peace with the church. If a leader is evil, a merciless official will be sent against him. In other words, if you are a leader, you should not be evil.

Proverbs 19:12 This verse teaches us that leadership sometimes must use authority, but his favor is like dew on the grass. When the king rages like the roar of a lion, it can give a godly lesson to teach the people to respect him and give him honor. Knowing that in the community or in the church, we need a person who practices justice and encourages a good life for all.

Proverbs 20:8,28 In verse 8, we are taught that when the leader comes out to the congregation or the community to judge, he winnows out all evil with his eyes. He keeps justice in order to give peace and good life to the people. Love and faithfulness keep a king safe. Through love, his throne is made secure. We need the leader's faithfulness and love from the people or members of the church. That type of leadership comes and makes people secure.

Proverbs 21:1 This verse says that the leader is in the hand of the Lord. He gives him light and a good way which God likes. The pastor's heart needs to be in the hand of God to give him direction. This is how we can lead the church.

Proverbs 22:11 To become a good leader, a pastor or bishop must love a pure heart, and his speech must be gracious. He will have the king or the leader for his friend. A pure heart is very important in our society where we live. A leader needs to be the type of person who expresses gracious words in order to build the church. Good words edify the community or congregation or people.

Proverbs 23:1-3 Verse 1 is the most important verse for me. We understand that when a leader comes, it is necessary to research or note well what is before you. In verse 2, it is saying, "Put a knife to your throat if you are a glutton." When we become leaders, it is very important to ask God to give wisdom and to be wise to keep your enemy in front of you. And as the last verse says, pay attention to the leader and don't accept his food, because it is deceptive.

Proverbs 24:21-22   In verse 21, Solomon teaches his son to respect the Lord and the king and not to walk in the direction of the rebellious because those two will send sudden destruction upon them. It is hard to imagine the calamities they can bring. When we are in this world, it is very important to fear our God first and then the leadership of the church or the country where we live. When we do it, we will receive the blessing from God and will become a friend of the leadership.

Proverbs 25:1-7,13   These verses are very difficult to write commentary about, but I understand that Hezekiah restored the temple, destroyed idol worship centers, and earned the respect of the surrounding nations. It is better to quietly and faithfully accomplish the work God has given us to do. As others notice the quality of our lives, then they will draw attention to us. It is often difficult to find people you can really trust. A faithful employee/messenger is punctual, responsible, honest, and hardworking. This person is invaluable, and he or she helps take some of the pressure off his or her employer. Find out what your employer needs from you to make his or her job easier and do it.

Proverbs 28:2-3,15-16   These verses teach us that for government or society to endure, it needs wise informed leaders. These are hard to find. It has many rulers. Each person's selfishness quickly affects others. When enough people live for themselves with little concern for how their actions affect others, the resulting morale rots and contaminates the entire nation. The leaders who came from a family where they were poor are like a driving rain that leaves no crops. If one leader is wicked, his form of government is not going to be impeached (he holds onto power). Use your authority to lead a people and the church. The last verse teaches us that the leadership which hates ill-gotten gain will enjoy a long life. A tyrannical ruler lacks judgment. We are pastoring the people to take them to the Lord.

Proverbs 29:4,14   Godly leaders are not greedy for bribes because it will tear them down. But the leader who makes justice gives a country stability. We need the pastor or bishop not to accept bribes. Rather, he should help to make good justice and a good life for all of the membership of the community or the church where he is a leader. If the king judges the poor with fairness, his throne will always be secure. All the godly leaders should remember to love and to make a good justice for the poor and the rich — all the people that are in our community where we live.

Personal Reflection

For godly leaderships, in my personal reflection, according to what I have learned from Proverbs, I understand the following:
1. We need wisdom from God first. I remember that Solomon son of David, when he came to take the king's place, asked God to give him wisdom. Wisdom is very important in our personal life and in our leadership in the church.
2. We need good counseling from our members to help us.
3. We need a leader to not betray justice with his mouth. Instead, he should keep out everything that can't help the church members.
4. We need leaders who detest wrongdoing.
5. Sometimes it is necessary for the leadership to use authority to teach and to make laws in the church.
6. We need leadership whose speech comes from a pure heart in order to share something which shows justice and knowledge from God.

My biggest challenge is to lead the church in a godly way using wisdom from God. God is telling me to change my behavior, by asking God to give me wisdom so I will lead well the church and my community where I live. For me, prayer is the only way to change behavior and to overcome many situations of life.

What I plan to do to make the situations in my family, church and community better is the following:

1. I will use the wisdom which I learned from the book of Proverbs.
2. Before making a decision, I will first ask counsel to help me make a good decision regarding everything I want to see happen (Proverbs 15:22).
3. I will be firm in my goal to have a pure heart and gracious speech (Proverbs 22:11).

Using this wisdom, I think that I will make the situation better. Blessings!

Barnwell Manjiche

Barnwell Manjiche (1986) lives in Mutare, Zimbabwe where he is a local church assistant. He has been involved in pastoral and evangelism ministry for 13 years. He is married to one wife and has a brand new baby daughter. His business experience for the past 11 years is in retail where he is responsible for buying and selling. His favorite hobbies are traveling and playing games. Barnwell's favorite Bible verse is Proverbs 12:11. His advice to young ministers is this: "I would like to take this opportunity to say to my fellow ministers to fear God, which is the beginning of wisdom. All young ministers should be able to work hard using their hands rather than expecting to be given everything by the church. To all ministers out there, you should understand that being a minister is a huge job in the whole world, and the devil is looking to destroy what is intended by God (Matthew 28:19). Lastly, watch out for other 'ministers' who are not fully born again."

Troublemakers
Proverbs 1:10-14

Audience: Teenagers

Commentary
Proverbs 1:10 Troublemakers do not start from an unknown or hidden path as teenagers, but they entice you to follow their path. The only key to success for them is when you give in to them.

Proverbs 1:11 Teenagers are usually carried away and follow troublemakers. This is because troublemakers clearly state their vision. When you follow them, you are aware of what you are getting into. Another point is that troublemakers target harmless souls, those who behave better than other teens.

Proverbs 1:12 As a teenager, troublemakers insist or praise you that you are macho, greater than anyone, and that you don't fear anything. The verse speaks of "let us swallow," meaning they are real troublemakers who are determined to achieve goals which are negative.

Proverbs 1:13 Troublemakers desire a life that is too easy to achieve, especially the love of valuables. As a teenager, you are tempted with the latest shoes, TV games, cell phones, and even the life of those on TV shows.

Proverbs 1:14 As a teenager you are afraid to be left alone, especially at school. What troublemakers do is that they give a purpose to follow them. Also, troublemakers demand your total dedication so that once you are in, you cannot quit.

Illustration
It was when I was 17 that I gave my life to Christ. Prior to that, I had met a very young boy my age on our way to a conference.

As a teenager, we became friends in a flash. Little did I know he was a troublemaker. After the conference, we became good friends. He then started enticing me to follow his way to an extent that I followed his way; in other words, we became troublemakers together. He told me we should drink until we no longer loved alcohol. It's like he gave me a vision which I wanted to fulfill, like it says in Proverbs 1:13, "we will get all kinds of treasure."

We continued with our troublemaking as we disobeyed our parents' advice. We became excited about our lifestyle of partying, drinking, and sleeping with girls. As a teenager, I was fooled because I didn't pass my "A" level with good grades. I then missed an opportunity to be at a university. Most people my age who chose wisdom instead of troublemaking have better lives today.

I urge each teenager to choose wisdom, for she will give you good friends that will encourage you to do good things and support your good paths. If anyone among you teens is a troublemaker, I urge you to embrace wisdom, for the time is still plenty to make up what you have lost.

Questions
1.   Would you kill someone simply to steal their phone?
2.   Would one of you be willing to be sick of cancer (or some other disease) because you want to share one purpose with troublemakers?
3.   Will I listen to my mother's advice or to my friends?

Additional Points
Proverbs 28:10 You will fall into your own trap.
Proverbs 28:17 You will be a fugitive till death.
Proverbs 1:26 Your trouble will catch up with you and laugh at you and mock you.

Sexual Temptation
Proverbs 22:14, 29:3

Audience: Businessmen

Proverbs 22:14 I would like you to understand that as a business owner, you are a target for sexual temptation. This verse is warning you that the mouth of a loose woman is a deep pit. You need God to help you resist her temptation.

Proverbs 29:3 As a business owner, love wisdom, and this will give you joy in return. You will honor God as your Father. But a companion of prostitutes squanders his wealth. In short, watch out for sexual temptation. You can lose all your wealth because of it.

Illustration
I did a survey of many business owners who are men. Normally, when they start getting profits and living a better life with flashy cars, clothes and phones, they are attacked by prostitutes who then offer sexual favours in return. One businessman within our community did the same by dating a prostitute. He lost all he had worked for, even ending up with a divorce. I urge you all to work closely with your wives and also to keep the words of wisdom to avoid sexual temptation.

Questions
1. Will you be a companion with prostitutes as a business owner?
2. As a businessman, will you flash and flaunt your wealth to women?
3. As a business owner, would you work closely with a woman other than your wife?

Sermon 52
Sexual Temptation
Proverbs 23:26-28, 29:3

Audience: Women

Proverbs 23:26-28   These verses talk about a prostitute or a wayward wife who is willing to give her body to any man. She is compared to a narrow well. In other words, getting caught by her is like falling down into a hole. I urge all women to be faithful and resist sexual temptation.

Proverbs 29:3   Proverbs is looking at a man with resources and married to a woman. The verse goes on to warn men to not have company with prostitutes which cause a man to squander his father's wealth through sexual offers.

Illustration
I have met a young woman in my neighborhood who was married to one of our childhood friends. This young woman had a love for upper class life, meaning she loved expensive goods beyond her level. She met a wealthy man at her work place who tempted her to be a supplier of his desires. This led her to sexual temptation, and nothing comes for free. Younger women, I urge you to love your husbands and live within your limits so as to avoid sexual temptation in order to gain silver and gold.

Questions
1. Would you continue with your job if your boss asks for sexual favors?
2. Would you squander the wealth of your husband or build him up?
3. If you want sex, would you get it from any men other than your husband?

Sexual Temptation
Proverbs 22:14

Audience: Mixed congregation

Commentary
Proverbs 22:14 Dearly beloved congregation, we need to listen carefully. The Bible is saying an adulteress exists within our communities. The verse goes on to say her mouth is a deep pit, and anyone who is under the Lord's wrath will fall into it. Everyone needs to watch out for an adulteress who can lead him to do bad things like sexual favors.

Illustration
Sexual temptation can tempt anyone in this church, meaning anyone with flesh and blood. This proverb urges us to watch out for an adulterer or adulteress who can fool you to follow his or her ways. Whatever comes from the mouth of such a person leads to sexual temptation, for it is within his or her nature. We need to store up knowledge, dear congregation, so that when the time of testing comes, we will resist the devil, and he will flee away from us. Let us all pray and remain in God's presence that we may not fall into temptation.

Questions
1. Will I befriend an adulteress?
2. If you meet one, will you take his or her advice?
3. Is sex allowed by God?

My Personal Reflection
Proverbs has been a blessing in my life. It talks of wisdom, and having wisdom is greater than anything I ever thought. Wisdom is sitting on a high point watching and shouting to me. I was

simple but very much aware of what sexual temptation was all about. As a wise man, I should watch where I go and whom I befriend to avoid sexual temptation. When I go home, I plan to address men, women, youth, and couples telling them what the devil does to lead them astray from the good of the high calling.

To my community, I will teach young boys and girls to watch out for an adulterer or adulteress. I will teach them how one can be tempted and led astray. I hope people see that my own family will gain more from my wisdom. I will organize 10 or 50 people of God to train them each and one of my family members in order to store up knowledge.

Sexual Temptation
Proverbs 7:1-27

Audience: Men

Proverbs 7:1-10 Every man in this audience is tempted sexually. All men have sexual feelings by nature. Proverb 7:1-10 warns men to watch out. We are instructed to keep words of wisdom and its commands, binding them on our fingers. This is important, because verses 9-10 talk of a woman coming to you by night dressed in a way that tempts you.

Proverbs 7:11-27 When a man is tempted sexually, the woman will give you the best treatment. Verse 13 describes how she took hold of him and kissed him. Men, you have to watch out for her. She has offers which only are intended to fulfill her sexual pleasures. Some of these women are married women who want to use you. Remember her house leads to the grave.

My Story
In our community, we had a powerful preacher who hosted all night prayers most Friday nights. He had a passion to do ministry work, but he made an error. As a pastor, your duty may require counseling. A woman in his own church needed more attention based on the size of her problem. He was not married. They decided to seek God in the mountain, just the two of them. Proverbs says, "My son, keep my words," but he forgot. He was tempted sexually. This led to the downfall of his ministry, and his failure was published in the press.

Questions
1. Would you pray with a woman in a private room?
2. Will you walk where there are prostitutes at night?
3. If a woman says to you, "Come to my house. I am alone," do you say "yes" or "no"?

The Value of Hard Work
Proverbs 10:4,26; 12:24,27; 15:19; 16:26; 18:9;
19:15, 24; 20:4,13; 21:17,25-26; 24:30-34; 26:14-
15; 28:19

Proverbs 10:4,26 Verse 4 is talking of a man or woman who does not want to use his or her hands. This means that it makes that person poor. It goes on to say a hard worker brings wealth through his efforts. Verse 26 is putting up a clear picture that one who employs a sluggard or lazy person shall be irritated, for he will always have an excuse. Assigning a lazy person is not a good idea. It's like having vinegar as your drink every day.

Proverbs 12:24, 27 Everyone who is a hard worker will surely be in charge, whether from being promoted or from expanding his work which will give him dominion to rule. Failure to be a hard worker will cause someone to end up being used by other people for money.

Proverbs 15:19 When one is a lazy person, you are hindered by your habits. Every time you want to do something you fail to do it. For example, lazy men do not want to work in the sunny weather. But when one is upright, you are determined, and you will certainly achieve.

Proverbs 16:26 This verse talks of one's desire to have things, meaning that desire causes one to work hard.

Proverbs 18:9 It's pointless for someone to spend time being angry and also arguing over petty issues, for it will not profit you at all.

Proverbs 19:15,24 Laziness causes one to follow bad habits. It even encourages you not to be a hard worker knowing nothing will come out of your life. Opportunities even come your way, but you will refuse them, resulting in nothing good happening.

Proverbs 20:4 This verse talks of a lazy man who does not work when everyone is at work like plowing, but when it's harvest time, the lazy man will not find any harvest in his field.

Proverbs 20:13 This verse encourages everyone to work harder. The more you like to rest, the poorer you become. The more you are dedicated, it will bring food on your table.

Proverbs 21:17 This verse is teaching discipline amongst the saints. That is, if you are a person who loves things of this world, such as partying and clubbing, it will make you waste your resources more. If you love drinking, expensive perfumes, or makeup, this will be a stumbling block to become rich.

Proverbs 21:25-26 When someone is lazy, we find it can lead to death. They never want to work. Even if they desire to have something different, they end up with the same. The lazy person will never have anything.

Proverbs 24:30-34 This portion of verses is teaching us that even if you have a field or capital, if you are too lazy to plow, cultivate or even apply knowledge in business, it is worthless. You will get nothing out of it. A major emphasis is that one should not sleep or slumber or even fold hands — this means being lazy rather than working hard. You need to be a hard worker for you to produce or gain capital interest and to avoid poverty and scarcity in life. We should learn from lazy people how they have suffered even when they have the resources with them.

Proverbs 26:14-15 A sluggard is compared to a door and hinge. He is waiting to be opened and closed by someone else. So is a lazy man. Everything in his life leads him to nothing as he loves his sleep. The sluggard is not willing to contribute or work, whether it is his energy or time. This verse is alerting us to watch our laziness, as it leads to nothing.

Proverbs 28:19 All hard workers are being given assurance by God that they will have abundant food when they till their land, when they invest or trade wisely. Surely there will be returns in your business. Again, this verse warns us to stop fantasies and get into the real world. Apply full knowledge and understanding on how to invest or farm, and abundance will follow us.

 WalkwithGod.com Publishing

Jevas Mapfumo

Jevas Mapfumo (1980) lives in Mutare, Zimbabwe where he has been active in pastoral work, evangelism, and church administration for three years. He has six years of experience in the manufacturing of household and industrial chemicals. Jevas is married and has three children. His hobbies are gardening and reading. His favorite Bible verse is Romans 8:28. His advice to young ministers is: "Having a personal encounter with God surpasses all our understanding."

Love and Friendship
Proverbs 13:20; 14:7; 18:24

Audience: Youth (13-30)

Friendship determines your destiny. Boys and girls, you should utilize your time well as a youth and walk and plan wisely. In order to achieve your goals, you should associate with friends of good reputation. Friendship really matters, and it determines your destiny.

If you read in the Bible from the book of Proverbs 13:20 , it says, "Whoever walks with the wise becomes wise, but the companion of fools will be destroyed." This verse is self-explanatory. It simply says if you walk with wise people, you become wise also.

Now this explains what I have said in my introduction that if you want to achieve, walk and plan wisely. If you have wise friends definitely you plan wisely. But on the other hand, if you associate with bad friends, shame will befall your life. Someone would want to know "why?" Because, my sister, if your companion sleeps around with boys, you will follow suit. This is because the people you spend a lot of time with influence your life.

Illustration
I would want to share with you a certain story that once happened in our village. There was a boy aged 16 years who was doing form 3 at a local school. He had a good reputation as he grew, but disaster came when he joined a bad crew of friends. These friends resided in the same village, but they had finished their secondary level studies. Many weekends they took this young boy and went with him to the township nearby. At first, they bought him soft drinks while they enjoyed beer and smoking cigarettes.

Time went on, and he began to try their drinks until he became a drinker and a chain smoker himself. He failed to complete his studies, and his life became miserable because of his bad companions. The Book of Proverbs 14:7 says, "Leave the presence of fools, for there you do not meet words of knowledge." The more you dwell with fools, you should not expect to get any words of knowledge. Fools are fools, and they have no good plans.

In concluding my sermon, I will refer you again to the Book of Proverbs 18:24, which says, "A man of many companions may come to ruin, but there is a friend who sticks closer than a brother." Good, close friends who stick closer to you will never ruin your destiny.

Questions

Now today as you go back home, I want you to ask yourself these questions:

1. What kind of friend is your friend?
2. What benefits are you getting from him or her that are positive?
3. With that kind of a friend, do you see yourself achieving your goals in life?

Love and Friendship
Proverbs 11:16-17; 27:8-10

Audience: Married men

A loving man walks with good friends. God wants us to love our wives as much as Christ did the church. So the secret is, a loving man should walk with good friends always.

In Proverbs 11:16-17, the writer says violent men get riches. This tells us that those men who cannot love and are not caring are violent. What is only in their minds is how they can get riches. They spend their time managing only their wealth. Mostly this kind of habit comes as a result of the type of friends one associates with.

Verse 17 further explains that a kind man benefits himself, but a cruel man hurts himself. You make a name for yourself. You can choose to be kind to your wife, children and society. Good friends will help you to achieve this. What is in them influences your character. This issue of friends has no age barrier. If you choose cruel friends, you also become cruel and spoil your name. By so doing, you hurt yourself. Be loving and walk with good friends.

Illustration
My brother-in-law is a soldier. He does not take beer and is very quiet. He failed to separate himself from his work mates to the extent that he had no good friends except his arrogant and rough-riding work mates. They are not loving and have no kind words for their spouses. They have extra-marital relationships. This resulted in my brother-in-law copying them. His first marriage broke up after one child had been born. Right now, he is pursuing another marriage because of very bad friends.

Now in conclusion, gentlemen, Proverbs 27:9 tells us that the sweetness of a friend comes from his earnest counsel. What I am saying is this: good friends are sweet and from them comes sweetness that in turn help you to be a loving husband, father, and man in society.

Questions
As you go back home, or when you are at your work places, just ask yourself these three questions:
1. Am I a loving man?
2. Are my friends good, and are they loving?
3. With these friends, what will my future be like, and will my own children admire my legacy?

Love and Friendship
Proverbs 25:16-17; 25:19,21-22; 21:10; 12:26

Audience: Children (5 to 12)

Love your neighbors and be friendly. Our God is a loving father, and we are all His children. Since He loved us, we should also love our neighbors, and we should be friendly to people.

The Word of God in Proverbs 21:10 says wicked people desire evil and their neighbor finds no mercy in their eyes. This means that God does not want children who desire evil things in their hearts. Instead, enrich your soul with love. Whatever you do comes from the heart, so if your heart is filled with evil material you produce that. But guess what? If it is full of love, and you always love abundantly, your neighbors will be happy.

If you are children of God, be friendly to your neighbors and the community around you. Proverbs 25:21 encourages you to give bread to your enemies when they are hungry. Imagine your enemy when you give him bread! That is a sign of love, because Jesus said that we should love our enemies and pray for them.

Illustration
I have a story to tell you. A young boy boarded a bus going to see his grandparents who lived 240 km from the town center. On his way, the bus was full. The boy was seated since he boarded it from town, but there were some standing passengers including a certain grandmother of 62 years. You know what? The little boy decided to stand and allow that granny to sit. Along the way, the bus had a breakdown. They were delayed for seven hours. Because of that, they arrived around 7 o'clock. The little boy was confused now and did not know which way to take from the bus stop since it was now dark. Guess what happened. The old lady also came off at the same bus stop, and she asked him

where he wanted to go. When he told her, this grandmother said she lived just next to the boy's grandparents. The boy was happy.

What helped him? It was his love towards elderly people, and he was friendly. Just as Proverbs 25:20 says, "Whoever sings a song to a heavy heart is like one who takes off a garment on a cold day." He didn't act like that toward this granny. Be good to people. Be friendly as much as you can and love everyone.

Proverbs 25:16 says, "If you find honey, eat only enough for you and don't take too much." Children, this tells us to think of others in whatever we get. Let us be friendly to them. Jesus asked his disciples at one time this question: "How shall they know that you are my followers?" He went on to tell them that through love for each other they shall know you.

Questions
I want you to ask yourself these questions:
1. Do I love my neighbors, and what do they say about me?
2. Am I friendly to everyone?
3. Is Jesus happy about me with the way I talk to my parents?

Love and Friendship
Proverbs 3:3-4; 10:12; 15:17; 16:6; 17:17; 20:6

Audience: Married women and elderly women

Be steadfast in love and faithfulness. Proverbs 3:3-4 encourages you to bind love and faithfulness around your neck. In other words, the writer is simply saying you should be steadfast in love and faithfulness. Verse 4 goes on to say that by doing so, one will find favor and good success in the sight of God and man. Ladies, one would ask me, "How can I find favor from God or my husband?" Here is the answer to that: by being steadfast in love and faithfulness.

Love covers all wrong doings. Proverbs 10:12 affirms this. But hatred stirs up strife. As a woman, you are the face of the house. For visitors to feel at home, there must be a loving wife with good hospitality. Strife is stirred up by hatred. You should avoid this and remain steadfast in love and faithfulness. Let us look at Proverbs 15:17. It says it is better to have herbs for dinner if they are done in love. Imagine a visitor being more comfortable eating herbs for dinner in your house as long as there is love than having a fattened ox with hatred. Women, be of good heart. Let your heart be an oasis of God's love where everyone can run to when they are feeling thirsty.

Illustration
I want you to look at this story that once happened. A certain lady worked for me at a restaurant as a cashier. She earned very little. The amount was not enough to look after her family, but she remained so faithful to that company. She did not take advantage of being a cashier to steal money. That company was still small and growing, but she did not complain. She loved the

customers, and that helped the company to grow. Unfortunately, she left employment when her husband got a better paying job. Time went by. That restaurant grew to be a very big entity, and they advertised a vacancy for an accounts clerk. That lady's daughter applied and was called in for an interview. You know what? On the day of the interview, the officers were interviewing people. After seeing her name and surname, they asked if she was related to this lady. She said, "That's my mother." You cannot believe this. The officers said, "You have passed the interview because your mother did it for you. Her faithfulness to this company helped it to be where it is right now, yet she got a little salary. So this is how we can pay her." That girl could not believe this, but that was that, because love and faithfulness had done it for her.

The Book of Proverbs 16:6 affirms that by being steadfast, love and faithfulness is atoned for, and the fear of the Lord helps us to turn away from evil. That lady could not steal because she feared God, and God indeed paid her unexpectedly. People may fail to appreciate your love and faithfulness, but God knows all your works. Be like a friend who loves at all times as Proverbs 17:17 says. Don't get weary. Be steadfast in love and faithfulness.

I will conclude my sermon with Proverbs 20:6. We have women who proclaim their own love, but faithful ones are nowhere to be found. Ladies, let us shame the devil and be steadfast in love and faithfulness.

Questions
When you get home, ask yourself these questions:
1. Am I faithful before God and man?
2. If I chose to be steadfast in love and faithfulness, will this help me in the future?
3. Who should I love and why?

Personal Reflection

Through all the scriptures which have to do with love and friendship, God has been teaching me the following things: Love is very important. To love is wisdom, and failing to love is lack of wisdom. Friendship is important also. Whom I play with matters before God, and choosing the right friends is wisdom. As God's minister, I should have agape love and be friendly to people around me.

When I return home, I will teach the congregation I am leading about the issue of real love which God is looking for. I will teach them that we do not love because we are told to, but it must be a heart issue. I will also teach people about the wisdom of God that surrounds the issue of love and friendship.

As for my family, I will take these lessons as a tool to try and unite the family at large. I want my family to understand the wisdom of God that was hidden from us concerning love and friendship.

The only way I can help my community with what I am learning is through practicing what I learned personally. When they question me, "Why are you like this now?" I will use that platform to reveal to them what God has taught me during Proverbs and try to change the community.

Jessie Masimo

Jessie Masimo serves in Bvumbwe Full Gospel Church of God in Southeast Malawi near Blantyra. She completed Credit 12 A Level and her Teacher Certificate at Machemba Full Primary School. She is currently retired from teaching. She is married to Kenneth with whom she has six children and five grandchildren. She is active in leadership at the national level as an adviser, having worked as the secretary of Ladies Ministries National Council. Jessie has planted several churches throughout her ministry including West Chipoka and Loilongwe. She has preached throughout almost every district in Malawi. Her favorite verse is Proverbs 15:22. Her hobbies include reading and singing. Jessie's advice to younger women ministers is this, "They should be faithful to God as well as to their families. They should bring up their children in the spiritual way."

The Call of Wisdom
Proverbs 1:20-33

Commentary

Verse 20 The door is open to acquire wisdom. Wisdom is always crying loudly everywhere for it to be heard (in the streets, in the noisy marketplaces, and in the entrance of the city gates).

Verse 22 Wisdom is pleading to the simple ones, scoffers, fools, and even those who hate knowledge.

Verse 24 Wisdom is always there, leading by the Spirit, stretching out her hand; but no one is paying attention.

Verses 25-27 Consequences follow upon disobeying. There is laughter, mockery, and a striking of terror.

Verses 28-30 One day there will be no answer. Even if you call and seek, you will not find help from wisdom because of your evil doings.

Verses 31-33 Without wisdom, one perishes.

The Safety Which Comes from Wisdom

Proverbs 3:1,13; 4:1-27

Audience: Youth

Proverbs 3:1 How can one get trust? Do not forget the teachings. Keep God's commandment. Be faithful always.

Proverbs 3:13 Who is blessed? The one who finds wisdom and understands it. The one who listens to God's instructions. The one who acquires knowledge and wisdom.

Proverbs 4:1 Who should hear? Sons should hear their fathers' instructions. Always be attentive. There is a gain of insight upon hearing.

Proverbs 4:10 What is the impact of hearing the Word? When you hear the Word, you must accept it. Words of wisdom increase the ability to do things. You are given an abundance of life upon hearing and accepting the Word.

Proverbs 4:13-14 How does wisdom safeguard? Keep instruction and be guarded. There's a better life upon acquiring wisdom. Wisdom will protect one from entering the path of the wicked and the ways of the evil.

Illustration

My grandson named Ken is 14 years old. He has been such a naughty boy who would not listen to my advice. He was taken up with peer pressure. He had no time to stay and assist with chores. All he knew was moving here and there. He was lacking wisdom, but God's timing is best. When I took time to pray and fast, God one day touched him. One day when he came home, he humbled himself and asked for repentance. I and my husband assisted him in prayer. He committed his life completely to Jesus. Now he is such a good boy. I love him.

Questions
1. Why is it important to take more time to pray for others than yourself?
2. How can we convert other people to know God?
3. What is the beginning of knowledge?

WalkwithGod.com Publishing

Work Smarter, Not Harder

Proverbs 6:13; 11:15; 17:18; 20:16; 22:26-27; 27:13

Audience: Mixed congregation

Proverbs 6:1 Do not work or act against generosity but against extending financial resources. Do not act in an irresponsible way which could lead to poverty.

Proverbs 6:2 It is important to maintain a balance between generosity and being a good steward.

Proverbs 6:3 God wants us to help our friends and the needy, but do not attempt to cover the cost of the unwise.

Proverbs 11:15 It is safer not to involve yourself in another person's debt; you may end up losing all that you have.

Proverbs 17:18 Avoid being a witness by putting up security for a financial debt.

Proverbs 20:16 To avoid being in trouble, get a deposit if you put up security for a debt if it's for a foreigner.

Proverbs 22:26 Do not agree to guarantee another person's debt.

Proverbs 22:27 If you can't pay, you may end up losing all your wealth.

Proverbs 27:13 Be careful; you may distress your relationship.

Illustration
One day a snake was running from a burning bush. So when it saw an eagle, it asked for help to be carried to a safe place. The

eagle carried it around its neck. Upon arrival, the snake decided it didn't owe the eagle anything. They quarreled long. At last, the snake ate the eagle. The snake forgot all the good things the eagle did. Let us learn to show mercy to those who show mercy to us.

Questions
1. Is it good for a Christian to entertain fools?
2. Do you reap where you did not sow?

Work Smarter, Not Harder
Proverbs 6:4-8; 10:5; 12:11

Audience: Mixed congregation

Proverbs 6:4 In order for one to achieve in life, there needs to be hard work. The Bible says that anyone who does not work must not eat.

Proverbs 6:5 Let us work responsibly so that our families do not suffer.

Proverbs 6:6 As Christians, let us refrain from the temptation of laziness by sleeping instead of working hard.

Proverbs 6:7 Take the example of ants using energy and resources economically. They work among themselves in harmony.

Proverbs 6:8 Those who labor themselves reap abundantly.

Proverbs 10:5 Time wasted will never be regained. As Christians, let us see time as God's gift. Do not lose your opportunity to work hard. Wise people harvest in the summer, but one who sleeps during harvest is a disgrace.

Proverbs 12:11 Wealth is a crown for the wise, but the effort of the fool yields only foolishness.

Illustration
Monkey and hyena were family friends. The monkeys invited the hyenas for a feast which they organized to take place on top of a fig tree. The hyenas were told to wash their hands at the river. When they came back, their hands were dirty and they

had to go again and again to the river until the feast was over. They were fooled because they worked harder and not smarter.

Questions
1. How can we make our families succeed?
2. Do you think lazy people will acquire a place in the Kingdom?
3. Can God help those who do not help themselves?

Work Smarter, Not Harder

Proverbs 21:20; 22:29; 24:27; 27:18; 27:23-27

Audience: Mixed congregation

Proverbs 21:20 People should learn about sowing for the future. God's people need to examine their lifestyle to determine if their spending is God-pleasing or self-pleasing.

Proverbs 22:29 Wise people are the ones who trust in the Lord. They are complete people. The wise shall serve the kings rather than working among ordinary people.

Proverbs 24:27 Christians, let us carry out our work in its proper order. It is possible to work hard and lose everything if the timing is wrong. God wants things to be done in an orderly way.

Proverbs 27:18 Be sure in all your planning, organizing, and working that you do not forget the people who have helped you. Those who tend a fig tree are allowed to eat the fruit.

Proverbs 27:23-27 The uncertainty of life should make us as Christians to prepare for the future. Let us have foresight by giving responsible attention to our homes. Thinking ahead is a duty, not an option, for God's people.

Illustration
Make hay while the sun shines. A good farmer prepares enough food for his herds during the summer so that when the rains come, he can give his herd delicious food. As Christians, we should be responsible stewards.

Questions
1. Why is it important to prepare for the next season?
2. What are the consequences of laziness?

Work Smarter, Not Harder
Proverbs 14:4

Audience: Mixed congregation

Proverbs 14:4 A person with no vision is always unable to make a living because he lacks something to work with. When you only live for yourself, your life loses its meaning. In life, we should learn to share with others in the faith. If your life is empty of people, it is useless. No man is an island. No matter how wise a farmer is, you still need strong oxen to work for the large harvest.

Illustration
I remember a certain man who inherited wealth from his father who died. He used the money so carelessly without saving it in the banks. He was committed to immoral behavior. Though he was rich, he used the money carelessly and became poor. He lacked wisdom. Remember as Christians, let us apply wisdom on a daily basis, for wisdom is God's delightful tool.

Questions
1. Can you remember a situation in which you did something without applying the wisdom from God? Did you succeed?
2. How often should one apply God's wisdom?

Lessons for Godly Leadership
Proverbs 13:17; 14:28,35; 15:22; 16:15; 19:12;
21:1; 22:11; 24:21-22; 25:13; 28:2; 29:4,12,14

Commentary
Proverbs 13:17 In Solomon's day, as a King, he had to rely on messengers who were trustworthy and reliable because wickedness would bring trouble.

Proverbs 14:28,33 A leader who is slow in anger has great understanding in such a way that wisdom rests in the heart of such a leader.

Proverbs 14:35 Wise leaders will always make a king happy, but he is angry with leaders who bring disgrace.

Proverbs 15:22 Godly leaders help others enlarge their vision and perspective. Seek out advice from those with experience.

Proverbs 16:15 When a godly leader is pleased, his happiness brings good life to people, and his favor flourishes to many like springs of rain.

Proverbs 19:12 When any leader becomes upset, his anger is like a roaring lion; but at the same time, when anger slows, he shows favor to remove anger.

Proverbs 21:1 Many of the godly leaders have been under God's control although they may not have fully realized it.

Proverbs 22:11 A leader who fears and trusts God has a pure heart. He becomes a king's counterpart.

Proverbs 24:21-22 It is good to advise children to fear and respect the Lord as well as the leaders. Let them not associate with the rebellious, because when revenge comes, it will affect them all.

Proverbs 25:13 Faithful leaders are trustworthy messengers who are punctual, responsible, honest, and hardworking.

Proverbs 28:2 For a government or a society to endure, it needs wise, informed, knowledgeable leaders who will bring stability.

Proverbs 29:4 Any leader (king) who is just and honest builds up the land, but he who demands a bribe destroys it.

Proverbs 29:12 A leader who listens to falsehood will be surrounded by wicked officials.

Proverbs 29:14 A godly leader must defend the poor fairly and rescue the needy children. His leadership will last forever if he does this.

Personal Reflection

I thank God for the teacher who assisted me in understanding the book of Proverbs. I have been moved and encouraged by the Scriptures that I have read, some of which I have never known before. I pray that God will inspire wisdom in my heart so that I can apply it in my ministry, family, community, and wherever I go in order to bring change.

My biggest challenge will be how to reach different target groups in the entire community depending on the types of leaders. I really feel that God has touched me, because I am now hearing a positive attitude to change my behavior. The Scriptures I read during the week will reflect in my life.

When one accepts responsibility to obey God, many obstacles follow. Like in the Book of Matthew 13:24 about the parable of the weed, when a man sows good seeds in the field, then someone comes to sow weeds. One may be failing to have full commitment to the work of God by being involved much in family and community issues, like funerals, sickness, or a lack of finances. These may bring obstacles.

These are issues that will never fail to attack anybody, just as Job was a godly man, but obstacles came his way which he never expected. But upon trusting, praying, fasting, and reading the Scriptures, you will overcome. I will keep on trusting God, always seeking for His wisdom, and the devil's plans will not have a chance on me.

The book of Proverbs will be on my table every day during evening devotions in my home for my family and friends. This will help my family, including my children, to acquire wisdom, which will help them prepare for their future. I want God to help me apply His wisdom in my business, to learn how I can manage my finances and even the type of food that I will feed my family in order to bring a change in my way of living.

As for my church, I will address the Scripture in the book of Proverbs during Bible study every Sunday morning targeting different groups. I will organize house cell groups, nights of prayer, and evangelism in order to reach the community.

I will address the book of Proverbs to the ladies during the National Convention for Women Ministry. This can change the nation targeting mixed groups, elderly and young women.

Illustration

A Story of an Eagle: An eagle is a strong bird which catches many other birds or animals it targets. That's why it will rarely ever miss a catch. One day, the chickens were at the house busy looking for food without knowing high up there was an eagle. It flew instantly down and scooped up a cock and took it. All the chickens ran away to hide. How does this relate? As ministers, we need to have a good plan with confidence to achieve a goal in order to grow in ministry.

Gladys Kaluba Mubiana

Gladys Kaluba Mubiana (1972) has been involved in ministry to youth, children and ladies for 24 years. She holds her Bachelor degree in Education and her Masters degree in Education Management. She is the author of the new Zambian national curriculum in Social Studies for grades 2, 3 and 4 (Oxford). Gladys is married with two children. She has been involved in small scale farming and trading for 20 years. Her hobbies include traveling and reading, and her favorite Bible verse is Psalm 119:11. Gladys offers this word of advice to young ministers: "Get a godly and mature mentor."

Sermon 67

Honesty
Proverbs 10:2; 26:18-19; Luke 8:15; Acts 6:3;
Romans 12:17; 13:13

Audience: Ministry Leaders

A person who is honest is one who is truthful, faithful and of integrity. Such a one can be trusted by people at every level. A husband, for example, would trust his wife with resources like finances, knowing that she would follow the budget by using the available finances on what would profit the family. Similarly, leaders, and generally Christians, should be of good character if they are to carry out their responsibilities. Nations, including the church today, suffer from issues of corruption and economic depression because of having leaders who are not honest. This, however, calls for transformation.

The church needs leaders who are selfless and who genuinely fear God. No leader can succeed in ministry without being honest. First of all, every leader should be trusted by his/her followers. So how can they trust a leader who is not truthful and has no integrity? How can such a leader command respect? Would members find it easy to carry out instructions given by such a leader?

Leaders look after souls, material and financial possessions, and natural resources, just to mention a few; and that is the more reason why they should be of high integrity. God Himself sent His Son, Jesus Christ, who demonstrated honesty in His ministry on earth.

A certain pastor stole money with his treasurer. Today, people have left his church, leaving him with only his family.

Proverbs 10:2 Who is talking? Solomon. Dishonesty brings death. Treasures should not be gotten unfaithfully. Uprightness gives long life.

Proverbs 26:18-19 Who does Solomon liken a dishonest person with? A madman. When you deceive your neighbor, you will not receive help from him/her. Be honest and good to your neighbors and ministry equally.

Luke 8:15 Who does the seed on a good soil in the parable of Jesus represent?   Someone with a noble and a good heart. Leaders should hear the word and retain it in order for their ministries to grow.

Acts 6:3 Who were chosen? Deacons. For what purpose? To distribute food to the widows and other needy people. Deacons need to have wisdom and be full of the Spirit. Such men would fear God while wisdom would guide them to make sound and intelligent decisions. We all need to be full of the Spirit and to have wisdom in order to be effective in ministry.

Romans 12:17   Who was being given these instructions? Leaders and Christians. Leaders who have integrity and are honest will live at peace with everyone. Everyone will be happy with an honest person and will support their ministry.

Romans 13:13 All transformed lives should be of high integrity. God will never entrust his treasures (souls, material possessions, and many other blessings) in the hands of dishonest men. People equally cannot trust you as a leader if you are dishonest. Dishonesty affects effectiveness in ministry. If your ministry is to grow and God is to enlarge your tent, embrace the Word and get wisdom from the book of Proverbs.

Discernment & Understanding
Proverbs 26:4-11; 27:22; 29:9

Audience: Children

Proverbs 26:4-11 Who is talking? Solomon. A fool is a bad friend. Avoid answering a fool. God does not like fighting

Illustration
Once upon a time, Mulenga and Kabwe lived in the same neighborhood. They played several games together and shared some sweets and mangos. As they grew a little bit older, Kabwe became hot tempered and would quarrel and fight with his friend Mulenga and others. Suddenly no one wanted to play with him, including Mulenga.

Mulenga was not happy that his good friend Kabwe had become proud and bad. He tried to talk to Kabwe about his behavior, but Kabwe insulted him in response. Mulenga's parents told him to stop playing with Kabwe because he was a foolish boy. Kabwe became lonely and unhappy. He would cry because no one wanted to play with him.

In conclusion, the friendship between Mulenga and Kabwe ended because Kabwe was foolish and a bully. As children, you must find good friends and be a good friend yourself. When you are angry, forgive your friends and do not fight. Be like Jesus who was a friend of children. He loved everyone.

Questions
1. What should you do to a bad friend like Kabwe according to King Solomon's advice?
2. Role play the story of Mulenga and Kabwe.
3. Draw a picture of Kabwe crying because he has no friends.

Sermon 69

Discernment & Understanding
Proverbs 16:16,22; 14:12,24; 19:2,8; 18:15

Audience: Teenagers

Proverbs 16:16,22 Who is talking? Solomon. Wisdom is better than money. Wisdom can give you money. Money cannot give you wisdom.

Conflicts and Disagreements

When two or more people have different opinions, disagreement erupts which may cause friction, such as verbal and physical conflict. As teenagers, you should know that conflicts are normal, because no two people are the same. For Christians, however, it is important to recognize God even in hard times. Many teenagers are in conflict with their parents, church leaders, and even amongst themselves.

What are the sources of conflict? Money. Roles (who does what). Recreation. Personalities (prejudice). Sex. Religion.

Solutions to conflicts include effective communication, flexibility, humility and prayer, wisdom and knowledge, and ground rules to govern a family or group.

Note: Unresolved conflicts can kill relationships. They lead to physical fights. They lead to abuse, misery and low productivity. They lead to a poor self-image, bitterness, depression, and even suicide.

Most teenagers argue about personality differences, sex and money. A teen who fears God and has gained knowledge and wisdom will avoid unnecessary conflicts. Wisdom would enable teenagers to follow instructions, respect other people's opinions, and work hard to improve their status.

Every family, community, school, or church has values and goals, and these should be respected. For the teenager who has no wisdom, however, it is difficult to abide by the values of the family, school, church, or community. Even to make a choice whether to get fast money or wisdom will cause personal and inward conflict.

As teenagers, find time to learn. Put into practice what you learn. Write down your vision and goals so that you are not distracted. It is foolishness to make quick decisions without thinking through the results. Take time to listen to elders without looking down upon them. You can also avoid fighting over little things by compromising and learning to give in for the sake of peace.

In summary, do not haste for money. Money cannot give you wisdom, yet wisdom and knowledge can give you money. It is wisdom that will make you avoid conflicts and disagreements that may injure you.

Questions
1. What is conflict?
2. Is it sinful to have conflicts and disagreements?
3. Which is most beneficial: money or wisdom? Why?

Discernment & Understanding
Proverbs 20:5,12,15; 21:11; 23:12; 24:3-4,7,13-14

Audience: Mixed congregation

Proverbs 24:3-4,7,13-14 Who is talking? Solomon is advising his inexperienced son. Wisdom is sweet to the soul. Seek for wisdom. Wisdom may also not be found. If it's found, there is future hope.

Proverbs 23:12 Who is talking? Solomon is encouraging. Make a commitment to knowledge. Seek and appreciate instruction.

Do not worry about tomorrow. To worry is not to be sure of what will happen next. One may worry about food, health, a job, a life partner, and so on. Who worries and why?

A husband who has no job may worry about shelter and school fees while his wife may worry about poverty and shame. Whatever the case may be, what does Solomon in Proverbs 24:14 say? Brethren, there is no need to worry, but instead seek to learn. Knowledge will give you survival skills that enable you to run a business that will give you money to enable you to provide for your family.

Men, women, and children should develop the heart of learning so that they can apply what they have learned. Surely then they will be able to live happily. Knowledge can be learned from those who have once passed through some issues. We call them role models. Hear testimonies and use those testimonies to your advantage. Books and videos can also be very good sources of information. For Christians, read the Bible, attend Bible studies, fellowships, and get involved in community work to get skills. Christians have hope in God the Creator. Proverbs 24:14 encourages us that wisdom, if found, gives hope for the future.

Wisdom can be applied to enable someone to make a sound decision that would take away worries. I am a very good example. Despite having a full-time job, I am an author, I sell clothes, and also rear cattle and goats just to make an extra family income to ease the pressure off my husband. These ideas came about after reading about the woman in Proverbs 31. I was just a teenager then.

At the time I was entering marriage, I was already involved in small businesses. My late mother played a very important role to get me started, being a very industrious woman herself.

Wisdom and knowledge will benefit you as an individual. They will empower you. When you seek knowledge and wisdom, therefore, you will have hope for the future. It will be foolish for you to worry about anything. Change your attitude and way of life. Give your life entirely to the Lord, and you will worry about nothing.

Questions
1. Why do people worry about the future?
2. How would you seek knowledge and wisdom?
3. If worrying is not a solution to problems, what practical steps would you take to find school fees for your two children?

Discernment & Understanding

Proverbs 10:13-14, 23; 13:14-16; 15:14,21,24;
14:6,8,15,18,24,33

Audience: Women

Proverbs 10:13,14,23   Who is talking?   Solomon is giving advice. Wisdom will come from the lips of a righteous woman. She will say things that will help people. She will store up knowledge. How? Through the reading of the Bible and other books. Through walking in the counsel of godly women. By being skillful and by putting knowledge into practice.

Proverbs 13:14-16 Who is talking? Solomon the king. Every woman should get teachings (have a mentor) and understand those teachings in order to get help. A prudent woman will act out of knowledge. Wisdom and knowledge will enable her to build a strong family and other relationships.

The best way to get wisdom and knowledge which will enable you to discern and understand is to get closer to God. This can be done through reading the Bible. You should read constantly and diligently for it to make a difference in your life.

I encourage every woman to read the Bible and write notes for future reference. Women, it is wise to find time for God. Find a quiet place in your home and a quiet time of the day, especially early mornings. Remember you need God's guidance and presence every day for a successful marriage, family, business, and so on. Every woman needs discernment and wisdom even to just attract the attention and love from her husband. These can be gotten from scripture when applied to one's life, from godly and more experienced women referred to as mentors, and even from practicing the skills attained.

No church or society can stand without women. Therefore, learn the Word of God and get knowledge and wisdom that will give you understanding. Meditate on the Word of God, as this will help you discern good from bad.

There was a woman whose husband started cheating on her. When she discovered it, instead of packing out, she bought her husband a very expensive suit. She told him how much she loved him, how handsome he would look in that suit, and how thankful she was for all the years they had lived together. She concluded by assuring him that she would never cheat on him because she was proud of him. This she said as she handed him the suit.

This act made the husband humble, and with his eyes full of tears, he knelt before her and confessed his sins. He promised never to cheat on her again as he asked for forgiveness. From that day, their marriage was a totally new one.

In conclusion, women must seek knowledge and wisdom, as these will give you discernment and understanding.

Questions
1. Why is it important for a woman to have discernment and understanding?
2. Is the sermon an instruction or a fresh revelation of something you haven't previously understood?
3. So what?

Personal Reflection
From the scriptures studied and generally from Proverbs chapters 1 to 11, I have learned that as a Christian, leader, wife, mother, and educator, I need wisdom if I am to be effective. To have wisdom, however, I should read the Bible and other books, listen to other people's testimonies, and spend more time with godly experienced men and women so that I get some knowledge from them.

Sermon 72

Giving and Accepting Counsel

Proverbs 9:7-9; 10:8; 11:14; 12:15; 13:1,13;
15:22,31; 17:14; 19:16,20,25,27; 20:18; 23:9;
24:5-6; 25:15; 27:5-7; 29:1

Commentary

This is a third paternal appeal from Solomon to his son. It is a call to fear God and act in wisdom. According to King Solomon, a son who lives in humility by keeping his father's teachings would live longer. The knowledge and wisdom gotten would make the son prosperous when applied. Using wisdom would allow him to use available resources to make more money. He would also be protected from getting involved in bad behavior like sex and drugs which would send him to the grave early.

In Proverbs 9:7-9, Solomon tells his son that some people are foolish and would not take advice from anyone. It would be wise for him to avoid such people in order to live in peace. However, he should encourage and give advice to the wise and humble who would in turn respect and love him. Advice is only appreciated by the wise, so it is a waste of time to give it to the fool.

Proverbs 10:8   As a caring father, Solomon continues to emphasize wisdom as a weapon for security whereas a fool by his own ruin of commands puts his own life in danger. This also means that it is not enough to receive commands or advice, but what is important is to accept that knowledge so that it benefits you.

Proverbs 11:14 Counselors are there to guide and to help people make wise decisions. It is therefore prudent to seek advice from wise and more experienced people.   Leaders should give guidance and advice to those who seek it truthfully.   Every leader should know that people out there look up to them and therefore should produce maturity and confidentiality. Always consult God in prayer so that no one is misled and so that wise counsel is given through the Holy Spirit.

Proverbs 12:15 This verse means that fools are too proud to hear and accept advice. Pride makes the fool blind not to see everything and not to separate good from bad. For a fool, everything he knows and decides is right, yet a wise person treasures counsel.

Proverbs 13:1,13 Children are encouraged to listen to their parents and take advice. No parent would mislead his child but wishes the best for him. Parents are more experienced than their children; that is why children should honor them. As children of God, we must know that He loves us so much and does not want us to perish. So we must listen and follow His commands. The verse also assures us that the wise who follow his commands shall be rewarded. For example, a girl who does not involve herself in premarital sex will not get pregnant outside of marriage.

Proverbs 15:22,31 Verse 22 recognizes the fact that no one on this earth knows everything, hence the need to seek advice by consulting more experienced people. It also means that for a person to achieve a goal, there must be planning. Failing to plan is planning to fail. Solomon therefore advises his son to plan and consult experts for guidance and interpretation. He goes on to say those that who heed and accept rebuke will definitely live, play, eat, and walk with the wise.

Proverbs 17:14 Quarrels should be avoided to prevent the production of painful and offensive words which may lead to serious disputes. It is wise to minimize and avoid quarrels in order to stop disputes. Water from a breached dam cannot be stopped from flowing, just as words from an angry and hurting heart cannot be stopped.

Proverbs 19:16 These are guidelines or principles of wisdom in the light of fearing God as the owner of life. The Scripture shows the elements of good life. The keeping of commandments will protect one from early death, for example being shot because one has stolen, dying from an STD or being cursed by people.

Proverbs 19:20 When we obey God, we get wisdom which helps us now and in the future. So we must not only obey God but also listen and accept advice from fellow humans who are more experienced than us.

Proverbs 19:25 This verse is also about principles of wisdom. Foolish people find it difficult to accept correction, yet an understanding wise person will learn and get more knowledge from the same situation. It is also about obeying God to get more knowledge and wisdom.

Proverbs 19:27 This verse is a parental advice to show how important it is to continue learning. The son is being encouraged to have a teachable spirit in order to gain knowledge which will guard his life and produce success. Developing an attitude of "I know it all" leads to foolishness and death. A humble heart learns. This is an appeal to all of us to humble ourselves and be teachable.

Proverbs 20:18 This verse means that before making major decisions, it is wise to seek advice. However, one should be very careful on whom to consult, as some people out of jealousy may frustrate your plans by misleading you. Let the people who advise you be mature and able to keep secrets. This means that counselors must practice confidentiality. For you to know such counselors, wisdom must be applied, or else you will consult fools who will destroy and hurt you. Equally, when you are consulted, be mature enough to keep secrets. This also means that everyone needs someone.

Proverbs 23:9   The son is being advised to avoid speaking to a fool who will not appreciate anything but find faults in any advice that will be given. A fool will not see any positive value or wisdom from counsel. Therefore, it is wise to avoid talking to him or her and probably just continue praying for such a one. The Holy Spirit who is gentle does not force us, but He steps aside when we refuse to listen. Let us listen, or else we will not have counselors.   The result will be going astray and not succeeding in what we do.

Proverbs 24:5-6   This means that wisdom is the source of strength. It empowers you to handle different situations. In fact, it gives you skills to handle difficult and simple situations or circumstances. There is a need to consult many wise people for guidance in order to succeed in all our plans. However, we need to choose these counselors carefully and with the guidance of the Holy Spirit, so that the wise and pure counsel, when put into practice, will enable us to succeed in all circumstances.

Proverbs 25:12   Wise words here are being compared to or likened to gold earrings which are of high value and should be treasured. Wise men's rebuke and advice should be appreciated because it is expensive. A person with wisdom and the fear of God can never advise foolishly, and therefore their words should be received with a merry heart to accept rebuke. So here there is a giver and a receiver. This image represents godly speech.

Proverbs 27:5-6   This is a paternal appeal for a son to uphold integrity for his own benefit. He is being encouraged to build strong relationships, be it with neighbors, relatives, and in a marriage. It is necessary to have friends and also to be friendly. Nevertheless, we should not be careless by trusting everyone. Some people pretend to love us when they don't. Their motive about us may be totally misplaced, so wisdom is needed. We usually do not like those who rebuke us and tell us the truth. However, we discover that when things are bad, those actually are the ones who love and care about us and not those who flattered us. A test is when we face trouble, some people who pretend to be close and caring abandon us. We must be very careful. We should also be helpful by not just using people for our own benefit. Love people and live at peace with everyone so that even when we need help, we shall go there without shame. In a marriage relationship, like any other, both parties should examine themselves.

Proverbs 27:7 This verse says something bitter is sweet to a hungry man, because what he needs is food without paying attention to the taste. A simple person who is seeking knowledge will look for it and appreciate it once found because he has use for it. When we hunger for the Word of God, surely it will find room in our hearts and will be of great use to our entire lives.

Proverbs 29:1 This verse is a warning that if we do not repent, we shall be destroyed and pay heavily for our shortcomings. Many a time rebuke and advice come, but due to pride and foolishness, people decide not to follow. In the end, they pay heavily. An example is a son who has been advised to stop taking drugs, and due to pride, he refuses to take that advice. A few days, months, or years later, he is sent to jail for 20 years. Similarly, we hear about hell and judgement, but some people decide not to take the message seriously and get saved. A day is coming when they will perish in the lake of fire. One may seem to be happy and doing fine, say in business, but as long as evil is involved, such a person one day will pay for it. This verse is an assurance that one day, the wicked will surely fall. We all need advice to succeed. Let us not be proud, but take and accept rebuke. Repent and turn away from all wickedness.

Personal Reflection
Reading through the Scriptures, God is leading and reminding me to get closer to Him so that I can gain more knowledge and wisdom that will help me succeed in all I do. Proverbs encourages me not to lean on my own understanding and to seek advice from more experienced people. Also, I am learning the

importance to plan and, in humility, present my plans to God for them to succeed.

The other thing I have learned is that I am encouraged to encourage others. As I seek counsel from those who are wise and mature, I should also give out counsel to those that seek it, not forgetting my children. I have been reminded to accept rebuke and correction no matter how painful and humiliating it may be.

My biggest challenge has been seeking counsel and advice on certain matters, especially within my local church, due to lack of confidentiality by most of the leaders. This makes me keep certain things to myself if I cannot ask my husband or daughter.

Through these Scriptures, God is telling me to learn to trust some people and also to help those who cannot keep secrets, as this may create a gap between the youth and the elders. The youth have so many unanswered questions, but they fear to consult the leaders. They end up making mistakes like unwanted pregnancies, drunkenness, resentment, and suicidal attempts to name a few.

I have also learned not to easily give up on people, especially youth and women. I see this from Solomon who kept teaching and advising his son. As much as I need to be helped, other people out there need my services and encouragement too. While others may just need counsel, others may need material and financial help. I should be able to share whatever God has blessed me with.

While I have served God for some time now, sometimes I find myself failing to obey simple instructions from God like, "Ask that one," or "Help that one." God has promised to give us what we desire, but sometimes I fail to wait upon Him and end up with anxiety.

I hope to continue reading the book of Proverbs and other books from time to time in order to increase my faith and wisdom. Counsel is also something that I will always seek. I will always pray and ask God to help me both give and accept rebuke and counsel for a victorious life.

Other Applications

Pride and lack of wisdom has caused misunderstandings and conflict at times in my family, local church, community, and nation. Some members of my family, church, community, and nation refuse to live by God's standards and end up being lazy and not contributing much to social development, peace, and harmony. I have some cousins who are quite lazy, destructive, and jealous. This is because they have ignored the instructions of God and live foolishly. They are irresponsible and want handouts. Their lack of necessities frustrates them.

At the national level, we have leaders who are selfish, corrupt, and lack wisdom because they have no fear of God. A lack of political will to improve the economy and citizens' lives frustrate citizens who end up losing hope. Such citizens no longer care for anything, which can be seen from the levels of violence, vandalism, garbage dumping, and verbal abuse, just to name a few. These problems affect families, the community, churches, and the whole nation at large.

These Scriptures are addressing the results of foolishness, pride, and lack of wisdom. They are also encouraging everyone to turn to God and seek wisdom which will change their mindsets. It is not easy to accept rebuke and advice, but life is about that. Let everyone seek and treasure wisdom.

To make the situation better in my community, I formed a women's club last year. During our meetings, we share skills which empower women to better their lives. We also share how to save money, how to raise responsible children, and how to work together and care for one another. Topics like stopping gender-based violence, child marriages, and keeping our environment clean are discussed, to name a few.

As an educator and author, I talk to pupils on some sensitive issues during Assemblies and even as I teach civic education. Some of the topics like family, respect, religion, and citizenship are reflected in some of the social studies books that I have written with the hope that people's minds can one day change.

At church, during our ladies' weekly meetings, we share and discuss the need to read the Bible and get involved in prayer and Bible studies to enhance our knowledge and to get closer to God. We always try to emulate the woman in Proverbs 31. Sometimes I talk to youth to encourage them to seek God and His wisdom and also to accept advice from their parents. In summary, it is not easy to change people's behaviors, but with God, all things are possible. One day we shall see change.

🐘 Luckmore Mudhluri

Luckmore Mudhluri (1990) resides in Chipinge, Zimbabwe where he has been active in ministry for two years with Chitepo Assembly in Manicaland. He also has worked in construction for five years. He is married to one wife. His hobbies include

watching television, playing the piano, listening to music, and studying the Bible. His favorite Bible verse is Psalm 125:1. Luckmore's advice to young ministers is this: "Be committed to the work of God in season and out of season. No matter what, there are challenges that may be faced in ministry. I encourage young ministers to believe that only God will make things to settle down."

The Cries of Wisdom and Folly
Proverbs 1:20-33; 9:1-6,10-18

Audience: Teenagers

Proverbs 1:20 In this verse, wisdom calls in order to give warning to people who do not obey God's principles. Parents should give advice to their children not to do fornication, giving them wise sayings. In this concept, wisdom is trying to alert people to these bad ways of doing things so as to follow a good path.

Proverbs 1:28 If people fail to listen when wisdom is crying loud in the streets, they will fall in their sins because of disobedience. However, whenever the troubles come and they try to find help or even try to call, no one will answer. They will not be able to find help, just as God refused to listen to Israel when the people sinned. When people find wisdom, they also find life and blessing.

Proverbs 1:29 This scripture illustrates that if people disobey the teachings of their parents, rejecting wisdom, they can be certain that consequences will attack them. Only fools are the ones who deny wise teachings. The Bible says fearing God is the beginning of wisdom. The teaching from this scripture encourages all groups of people to submit themselves whenever they are being taught about wisdom in order to be fully impacted by it.

Proverbs 9:1 Both wisdom and folly have built their houses to which humans are invited. Seven pillars in this scripture refers to the perfection of wisdom's work.

Proverbs 9:2 In this scripture, the adulteress mixes wine with spices to make it tastier. She calls from the highest point of the city.

Proverbs 9:10 Fearing God is the beginning of wisdom. If you fail to obey God, He won't care for your business. Anyone who hates wisdom loves destruction.

Proverbs 9:11 This scripture is saying when people obey wisdom, the number of their days will be increased by God. This means God blesses people who obey Him.

Illustration

I have been a youth leader for the past two years. A proposal was made to the teenagers or youth from each local assembly to contribute food which was to be allocated for the conference. Everyone agreed to the proposal, and the dates were set for the occasion. On the day of the conference, just a few local assemblies contributed food. There was only enough food for one day, when it was supposed to be enough for the full three days of the conference.

The wisdom that I had acquired from God gave me the idea of having people contribute in the form of an offering. People gave offerings, and that money was used to sustain the conference for the remaining two days.

Questions

1. Why do you think wisdom is very important in our lives?
2. How do you identify that someone is lacking wisdom?
3. Do you think people who have wisdom go to hell?

Correction and Discipline

Proverbs 15:5,10,12,32; 19:18

Audience: Women

Proverbs 15:5,10,12,32 These scriptures give advice to a son to obey the teachings of his father. They tell us that whoever listens to and heeds correction shows prudence. Anyone who hates correction will die. It encourages the son to seek correction from the wise. Fools ignore discipline and despise themselves.

Proverbs 19:18 When a son is being disciplined, he will obtain hope. Disciplining or correcting a son doesn't lead to death.

Illustration

There was a girl who grew up without being given correction or discipline whenever she did wrong things. However, this affected her when she became a mother of a house. She didn't seek advice from others and refused to be corrected on how to be helpful and how to take care of her family. She didn't even know how to cook and do basic things like laundry. Therefore, the marriage was destroyed due to lack of wisdom.

Questions

1. What will happen when someone hates wisdom?
2. Why is wisdom so important in our daily life?
3. What do these Proverbs mean in your life?

Sermon 75
Correction and Discipline
Proverbs 20:30; 22:6,15; 23:13-14

Audience: Business Owners

Proverbs 20:30 Blows and wounds cleanse away evil. This means that stern punishment exists to remove the evil. Proverbs often talks about fools whose backs are beaten.

Proverbs 22:6,15 Train a child in the way he or she should be as a grown up. Failing to train a child when he is young means that when he is grown up, it will be difficult for him to be corrected. Hating a rod to discipline a child means that child is not on the heart of the parents.

Proverbs 23:13-14 A child should not be withheld from discipline. Punishing a child with a rod doesn't mean the child will die. Punishing a child is serving the child.

Illustration
A businessman from my community owns a big shop. He put his son in charge to manage his shop. Due to lack of wisdom of the son, he always took money from the business for his life of luxury while spending much of his time with prostitutes. However, the business declined because he was failing to manage it. Therefore, his father regretted later failing to discipline his son from doing bad things. Wisdom is the key of life. Accepting correction from parents will make children wise. In my family, my brother always neglected the teachings of our parents when they tried to give him guidance in life. He wouldn't listen. The Bible says anyone who hates wisdom loves death. He managed to associate with a drunken crew of gangsters who were bank robbers. My brother ended up in jail because he hated to be disciplined by our parents and hated even to be corrected. As I speak, my brother is in prison.

Questions

1. What were the major things which caused the decline of the businessman's shop?
2. Does God love people who hate wisdom?
3. What are ways good parents can raise up their children?

Personal Reflection

I have learned that as a child of God, in order to succeed in everything in my life, I have to seek wisdom from Him first. In Proverbs 9:10, it says the fear of the Lord is the beginning of wisdom and knowledge of the Holy One is understanding. I learned also that when I get wisdom, it will reward me. Only the mockers will suffer. The book of Proverbs also encourages me that if I work hard, it brings wealth. Lazy hands bring poverty. When I return home, I will teach people that God expects everyone to have wisdom in everything that they do. However, I will teach them also to listen to their parents in every aspect so that they will be corrected when they are disciplined.

Correction and Discipline
Proverbs 3:11-12; 10:17; 12:1

Audience: Mixed congregation

Proverbs 3:11-12   This chapter is giving a warning that the righteous are not always prosperous in times of testing and affliction. God is teaching as He disciplines His people.

Proverbs 10:17 God is talking to His people that everyone needs wisdom so that he will be able to be corrected in what he does. He illustrates this by saying that when you hate correction, you can lead other people astray.

Proverbs 12:1 This scripture illustrates that God wants people who love discipline in order that they will have knowledge. This verse ends up by saying that when a person hates discipline or correction, that person is stupid.

Illustration

There was a certain guy from a local church who was a present worshiper but who was also a drunkard. Whenever he went to church, he would drink beer. Most of the people in the church tried to correct him most of the time, but he didn't listen. He hated correction when he was doing wrong things. One day, God disciplined him in front of the congregation by causing him to vomit the beer that he had drunk, and he became ashamed.

What I learned from my story was that God rewards those who obey His commands or principles that He has given to us. I had been taught by my pastor about the giving of offerings and even tithes in the church. Before, I hated the principle of giving. However, by the time I had been corrected, God rewarded my business to a great standard.

Questions

1. What are the results of not obeying correction?
2. What do you understand by the term "discipline"?
3. Is it a must for the congregation to give offerings in a church?

Correction and Discipline
Proverbs 13:18,24; 14:9

Audience: Teenagers

Proverbs 13:18,24 A father who is talking is trying to give wisdom and advice to his children. Poverty and shame is caused by not listening to the advice given. The father encourages them that whenever they obey correction, they will be honored. Fools detest turning from evil because they hate correction. Rewards are only given to the righteous, and injustice sweeps it away. The father who spares the rod hates his son. When he disciplines him, it means that he loves him.

Proverbs 14:9 Whenever a father tries to amend his son in his evil ways and that son mocks his father, it means that the son is a fool. Only goodwill will be found among the upright.

Illustration
In my community, there was a guy who was from a rich family, but he loved fornication and disobeyed his father's advice. One day, his father decided to chase him away from the house, but he decided to give him some of his wealth to make sure his son would survive wherever he was going to stay. As the time passed by, the boy recklessly spent everything that he had with prostitutes, and he ended up starving because everything was gone. He had come to poverty due to neglecting his father's teachings. This story teaches everyone to obey the teachings of our parents and to learn to be corrected.

Questions
1. What will happen to the fools when they fail to change their ways?
2. Write down the results of lacking discipline.
3. What is a good man supposed to do to his children?

Living with Integrity

Proverbs 13:6; 15:26; 16:7; 17:13; 18:3; 19:29; 21:8,12,16; 22:8,21; 24:8-9; 26:1,3,27; 28:18; 29:10

Commentary

Proverbs 13:6 When people are being righteous in the way they live in society, they will be protected by wisdom.

Proverbs 15:26 God wants people with good manners who always seek good things to please Him. God hates the way wicked people think.

Proverbs 16:7 This chapter says that when a man lives in the community in a way that others admire and that pleases God, God makes his enemies to love him in the community.

Proverbs 17:13 This Scripture says that when people fail to do good things to their neighbors, that wicked person can never live with peace in his house.

Proverbs 18:3 When wicked people come, they bring contempt, and also the wicked show contempt for God's ways. This leads the people in society to know that they are wicked.

Proverbs 19:29 The prize of the wickedness of scoffers is ready for them. This means that the judgment of evildoing is ready to be given to the scoffers. Also, the fools will be beaten on their backs.

Proverbs 21:8 The ways of the people who do evil is crooked. People who love to walk wickedly and do evil things won't prosper. The ways of the righteous are upright.

Proverbs 21:12   Righteous people are supposed to do good things to the wicked to make them repent from their evil ways.

Proverbs 21:16   When righteous people admire the works of the wicked and then start to walk in their ways, their end will be like that of those doing evil. They won't prosper. It will also be death.

Proverbs 21:21   When a person pursues righteousness and all the good works, that makes the community happy, and he finds honor from the Supreme God.

Proverbs 22:8   What is being sown is what will be reaped. When people sow injustice, they will reap trouble; and even his anger or his rod will fail and not prosper.

Proverbs 24:8-9   The people who do evil plans will be called schemers, and the thoughts of the mockers will be regarded as abomination to mankind.

Proverbs 26:1   Only the righteous will be honored during times of summer, rain and even times of harvest. Their honor will not be suitable for the fool.

Proverbs 26:3   God is ready to punish the fools with a rod by just beating them on their backs. This means that God doesn't like fools; He intends them to be disciplined by a whip.

Proverbs 26:27   Evil people will be trapped in their own evil deeds. Whenever they dig pits, they fall in them, and the stones fall on the top of their own heads.

Proverbs 28:18   Those who have bad manners and are wicked will be trapped in their evil ways, and they will fall in them.

Proverbs 29:10   Only wicked people always seek to destroy the righteous people. However, the righteous always seek to be righteous for the rest of their lives.

William Mumba

William Mumba (1973) lives in Lusaka, Zambia where he serves in pastoral ministry with a new church plant (Kabanana Compound Deliverance Centre). The church is in its first year and is currently running 70. He has eight years experience in church administration. William also is involved in a small-scale hardware business. He is married with eight children. His favorite hobby is reading Christian literature. William's favorite verse is Matthew 28:19. His advice to young ministers is this: "All ministers in the church globally should commit themselves to the great commission. Jesus' assignment is omitted in the ministry. What is happening in local churches is that ministers are only teaching to those who are within the church."

Justice
Proverbs 12:17; 29:28

Commentary

Proverbs 12:17 Justice is defined as the quality of being just and fair in domestic and legal affairs. Here, the philosopher urges the congregation to acquire wisdom, because this is the truth that enables both parties to reconcile amicably. Therefore, one who stands in between must testify honestly according to what transpired on the scene without favoritism or corruption in order to avoid making life worse.

Wisdom has to be applied through speaking the truth, and every word that comes from the mouth must be beneficial to the community. On the other hand, what is deceit? It is dishonest or fraudulent words, the telling of lies for personal gain. The witness who tells lies or is dishonest destroys others with perverse words. A false witness creates his/her own shame.

Proverbs 29:28 The source of justice is from the Lord. Fairness means the congregation should hunger for it, asking God to expose clear insight upon disputes. Solomon asked for wisdom in order to pass justice between parties. The case was not easy, but God granted him what he requested. Justice is not an easy thing. We need to seek wisdom or justice for secular authorities, but in the true essence, it is God who gives it to rulers.

Illustration

Before I came to understand justice, I used to work as the Co-operative Secretary at Mandarin Market. One day two traders brought an issue that was very complicated. Both of them were fighting over a boyfriend. A man who was married with children used to come to see them and was having an affair with both of them. However, each did not know about the other. The argument became so hot that all the other marketers were concerned and were demanding justice.

I was given the platform to mediate and pass fair judgment against what they did according to the Co-operative bylaws. One of the culprits came privately to me with a brown envelope containing money in it. We talked, and I accepted the bribe.

When the day of the case came for settling, because of a corrupted mind, the verdict was not fair to the other lady. I accused her of misbehaving, painting a bad picture of her. Also, I ruled against the woman who did not bribe me.

Wisdom was crying but I did not listen to her. I did not serve my community better. I only brought outrage between the parties. After realizing what I did, I apologized to the lady I wronged. She accepted my apology, and today we are on good terms. I perceived wisdom, and the community appreciates what God has done.

Questions
1. How do you pass judgment in your family and in the community at large?
2. Do you accept bribes the way I used to do before I grasped wisdom?
3. Are you willing to seek wisdom as silver and gold?

The Benefits of Self-control
Proverbs 22:24-25; 23:29; 25:8

Audience: Congregation

Proverbs 22:24-25 The benefit of not making a friendship with an angry man brings competency and integrity in the congregation because the individuals are disciplined and thus understand the consequences of anger. Anger results in dividing the church, disunity, and fighting within the members. A disciplined and self-controlled person brings harmony among the believers and congregation.

Proverbs 23:29 A person who loves alcohol has these characteristics mentioned which easily ruin the community. The congregation may realize that the wounds that they are experiencing are painful because some time back, someone lacked discipline and self-control.

Proverbs 25:8 A disciplined and self-controlled believer must not haste to settle his dispute before the secular court because the just and wise people shall judge the world, not the world to judge the believers. The benefit of self-control here is that you avoid shame from your neighbors.

Illustration
The king of the jungle called all the wild animals to a meeting. The purpose of the meeting was to settle an argument between the animals that were living on land and those that resided in the water. They believed that the animals should have one home, either on land or in the water. This meant that either the land animals or the water animals would have to migrate. The meeting took several days, weeks, and even years without a final resolution. The answer has not yet been found, so the animals agreed to keep living the way they had been living.

Questions

1. Do you want to judge others before you judge yourself?
2. How do you settle disputes as a congregation?
3. How do you handle critical issues? Do you give enough time to resolve it?

The Benefits of Self-control
Proverbs 14:15-16; 22:24-25; 25:28

Audience: Youth

Proverbs 14:15-16 Life is a journey that needs steady strides. A young man must examine his short, middle, and long-term plans. Self-control and discipline distinguish between the simple and the wise. The benefit of the prudent is that they guard their steps daily before taking any action. They are thinking about the present, near future, and distant future for their progress and challenges. A thought that is applied positively produces good results. It takes the prudent to attain goals. Being cautious in every step in this world is very important, because many turn from good to evil ways. Competent youth avoid the foolish and reckless life since life is not reversible, nor can you add a single hour to it.

Proverbs 22:24-25 Youth must select good friends who will be able to progress him in life. Discipline upon oneself can benefit the community: children, youth, and adults. Group influence that leads to delinquency is reducible if the youths do not associate themselves with unwise youth.

Proverbs 25:28 Proverbs' emphasis on self-control or discipline is paramount because the majority of youths lack it. Contemporary generations should come back to the drawing board in order to benefit in life. The man without self-discipline is compared to a city broken into and left without walls.

A city is a wonderful place where all activities take place, for instance modern attire, soccer, films, and leisure. These are the things the youth crave, and all western cultures expose their youth to these things. But a precaution is revealed: the precious body will die due to the lack of self-control and discipline. The consequences are sickness, dying young, lack of wealth, etc.

This is like the fall of the walls of the city. He who does not manage his spirit is someone whose destiny leads him to destruction.

Illustration
Once upon a time, there was a sheep that used to stray from the flock. One day the vicious lion saw it and took advantage of the situation. The hungry lion ran after it, and it was bruised and fell to the ground. When the lion was about to kill and devour it, the shepherd who owned the sheep shot the lion right away in the head. From that day, the stray sheep learned a great lesson. The sheep understood self-control.

Questions
1. How do you want to benefit in your life?
2. When are you supposed to respond to wisdom?
3. Do you listen to the voice of wisdom daily?

Sermon 82

The Benefits of Self-control

Proverbs 14:17,29; 15:18; 16:32; 19:11,19; 29:8,11,20,22

Audience: Mixed congregation / Subject: Anger

Proverbs 16:32 Self-control against anger controls the situation that seems to be disturbing, mainly to those who depend on physical powers and even those who crave for things.

Proverbs 15:18 The causes of strife can be controlled by a man who is able to manage his temper. The one who brings peace and quiets contention is one who is slow to anger.

Proverbs 14:17,29 When someone acts hastily or has a bad temper, his foolishness is evident before the people in the community or churches. This person who plans bad things against others is not loved by the community. Whoever is slow to anger has great understanding.

Proverbs 29:8 Quarrelsome men bring or cause problems to the friends and neighbors who stay close to them. Wise men bring peace, for they are peacemakers.

Proverbs 29:11 There is no peace when a fool opens his heart, mind, and mouth. He produces anger. A man who is wise is able to guard his emotions.

Proverbs 29:20 The man who babbles in haste produces helpless and meaningless words. A fool is better compared to him.

Proverbs 29:22 Sins are committed mostly by the man who fails to control his anger which results in dissension. Patience is the antidote for anger. But he who has a hasty temper exalts folly. Great understanding is exhibited by a man who controls himself against anger. A man's folly is known when he fails to control his temper.

Illustration

Once upon a time, Mr. Sheep and other tame animals wanted to settle an argument that brought confusion and disunity in the village. The problem was that the domestic animals wanted to choose a king in the village, but the dog and the goat started fighting for the position. The goat was beaten to the extent that he had severe internal and external injuries. The meeting was postponed to another date. Some animals proposed that Mr. Sheep should help to act as a leader as they were waiting for the goat to recover from the injuries that the dog inflicted on him.

Questions

1. How do you react when someone annoys you in the congregation?
2. Do you think about others before you lose your temper?
3. Do you give yourself enough time when someone insults you before you act angrily?

The Benefits of Self-control

Sermon 83

The Benefits of Self-control
Proverbs 23:19 21 29,35; 20:1

Audience: Men

Proverbs 23:19   The wise man exercises control against the desires of his flesh. Thus, he daily lives the life he is supposed to live.

Proverbs 23:21   People who are selfish and fond of drinking illicit beverages and who do not plan will soon fall into the trap of poverty, and the little slumber will cost them.

Proverbs 23:29   The drunkard expects the things that Solomon mentioned. The wounds resulting from beer require medication, but medicine is costly. It also can lead to prison. Strife also has its consequences, such as ending up in prison or courts. Everything mentioned is caused by drinking beer.

Proverbs 23:35   A drunkard does not acknowledge or understand whatever happens during and after drinking. He even tries to strengthen himself without knowing the repercussions.

Proverbs 20:1   Wine is the dangerous stuff that makes a man do unreasonable things, and whoever indulges in such activities loses direction.

Illustration
There was a shepherd who used to tend the flock on the green pasture near the brook which flowed and gave fresh water to the flock. The flock was well nourished and healthy. One day, Mr. Sheep left the place where he used to graze with his fellow sheep, and he joined the group of goats which were living far from the rich place. These notorious goats used to feed on garbage. When Mr. Sheep reached the place, it was not what he

178   WalkwithGod.com Publishing

ever expected. He realized that he was totally lost. One surprising thing that he saw was that the goats were sleeping outside, drinking dirty water, and the one who was tending them always beat them because of their behavior.

Fortunately, the good shepherd was searching for him. Eventually the shepherd found Mr. Sheep among the troublesome animals. The good shepherd took him back home.

Questions

1. What kind of friend do you associate with?
2. What are the dangers of drinking beer?
3. How can you avoid those who drink or how can you stop drinking beer if you already do?

The Benefits of Self-control
Proverbs 21:5

Audience: Youth / Subject: Business

Proverbs 21:5 Diligent men plan like small ants. They gather their food in Summer, preparing themselves for the future. The diligent use simple machines like tractors and animals to work a big portion in order to have plenty of produce. But those who do not plan well come to poverty. Even the little they gather is lost.

Illustration
The sheep on a certain farm planned well for his future. He had a long-term and a short-term plan. The long-term plan was scheduled for ten years. He saved some money every month, 20% from his proceeds. After a year, he invested the interest from his account. After ten years, Mr. Sheep bought a tractor that helped him to make the work on the farm easier.

For his short-term plan, Mr. Sheep wrote down things he needed like medicine, food, rental, etc. Some of the other animals were too busy watching and enjoying the very day they were living. They lived without knowing that there is a tomorrow.

Questions
1. Do you plan for tomorrow?
2. How do you plan?
3. What parts of your life are important to plan?

Lessons for Godly Leadership

*Proverbs 13:17; 14:28-35; 15:22; 16:10,12-15;
17:7,11; 19:12; 20:2,8,26,28; 21:1,21-22; 22:11;
23:1-3; 25:1,7,13; 28:2-3,15-16; 29:2,4,12,14;
30:1-9*

Audience: Men

Proverbs 13:17 A leader who represents the King works faithfully, for he represents and serves in the ministry. He does this not for himself to be served by the people but, on the contrary, to serve others. Some wicked ministers work for self-benefit and egocentric goals which result in reckless or malicious behavior that causes discomfort in others.

Proverbs 14:28-35 The sign of good leadership is known by the subjects loyal to him and the majority who are pleased with the ruler's oracles. The same applies to the subject of the servant who works under the king's orders. Godly leadership is about servanthood that is done wisely. Service before the King is measured by humility, commitment, and competency in order to find favor before Him. Lordship over the King degrades the one who equally compares himself with the King. While reflecting on these verses, I realized that the interaction between the subjects and the king is about loyalty, commitment, and competency to the authorities who are above me. I also have observed that good leaders are loved by their subjects. My greatest challenge in obeying God is that I give some excuses.

Proverbs 15:22 Godly leadership desires a multitude of advice from elderly, God-fearing leaders who are able to attain the planned goal. Men of purpose counsel one another for the edification of the body of Christ and the community at large.

Proverbs 16:10,12-15   Anyone who needs to be loved by the king should hate sin, because the king requires righteousness on his throne. Therefore, truthfulness before the king is essential, because the king doesn't tolerate lies that will lead to death. Obedience pays.

Proverbs 17:7,11   The true leader or ruler depends on honesty and justice, which means deception is bad. The man who rebels goes the wrong way.   Every evil action is punishable by a merciful leader who doesn't tolerate evil.

Proverbs 19:12   The king or leader punishes those who disobey, but his favor is imminent on those who are obedient.

Proverbs 20:2,8,26,28   Whenever a king gets angry, one risks his life. The king psychologically knows the evil that one has done. The leader exercises punishment upon the evil ones. Love is the key to keep the throne secure.

Proverbs 21:1   The Lord is sovereign. He uses leaders and kings according to His will.

Proverbs 21:21-22   The wise man who pursues righteousness and love prospers because he is honest when doing his work and motivating others.

Proverbs 22:11   Purity wins the king's heart. Leaders need wise friends, those whose speeches are not twisted.

Proverbs 23:1-3   Good reputation is more worthy than food. Good relationships should be a priority.

Proverbs 25:1,7,13   It is better to call someone privately for correction than to expose him before the leader. The trustworthy messenger does what the leader says.

Proverbs 29:2   The righteous need to work in state offices as politicians in order to change irregularities, bring transparency, and to stop the activities in which the secular wicked men are exploiting citizens.

Proverbs 30:1-9 To become poor or being in the state of poverty might cause someone to steal, but having enough is good.

Illustration
In the thick jungles of Africa, the cold weather of the month of June caused a well-known animal called a porcupine, a thorny animal, to want to warm himself among other animals. When it started embracing other animals in order to warm himself due to the cold, he pricked other animals with his thorny body. That caused the pricked animal to leave the porcupine. Eventually, the porcupine was left alone, and as a result he died from the cold.

The story illustrates ungodly leaders who claim themselves to be godly leaders in the church. These leaders always harm others with wicked sorts of activities when their fellow men want to learn more godly things. They use evil ways to retard the converts. Their motives are centered on material gain. The godly leaders, however, serve others rather than exploiting others.

Questions
1. How does godly leadership serve God?
2. What are the qualifications of godly leadership?
3. Why is godly leadership so important?

Craig Thompson

Craig Thompson (B.A., M.Div.) resides in Cleveland, TN where he wears many hats. He has served in various ministry capacities, including children's ministry, youth and adult classes, evangelistic work, drama ministry, music ministry and puppets.

His current ministry focus involves mentoring and life development. In 2010, Craig pioneered the 52 Godly Men and 52 Godly Women projects with his own children. In 2017, he launched The Mentoring Revolution, a mentoring curriculum for churches and small groups which is designed to provide a framework for intergenerational ministry.

He also owns and operates Caldwell Global Communications, Inc., a company specializing in solutions using Internet technology. Through his technical work, he has provided practical communications solutions to churches, businesses and non-profits on the six major continents.

Craig is married to Deana with whom he is raising six children. His hobbies include reading, gardening, photography, music, writing and playing with his family. One of his favorite verses is Romans 11:36. His advice to young ministers is: "Make an intentional choice to seek out mature mentors. Don't wait for them to come to you. Be willing to be different. World changers don't think like everyone else."

For speaking invitations, contact him at PO Box 2605 / Cleveland TN 37320-2605 or craig@walkwithgod.com.

 WalkwithGod.com Publishing

Comments

Did you enjoy this book? Did a particular sermon seem to meet your need when you read it? Do you believe that God spoke to you about your life while reading one or more of the sermons? If so, we would really enjoy hearing from you. To share a comment on this book or a story about how it helped you, send us a note at: proverbsbook@walkwithgod.com.

Please visit us on the Internet at walkwithgod.com where you can find more resources.

To support our ministries of leadership development, training, mentoring, evangelism, and writing more books and curriculum, visit this URL:

https://www.walkwithgod.com/giving

Errata

A list of corrected errata is maintained at:

https://www.walkwithgod.com/proverbsbook

The publisher requests that any additional errata be sent via the form on that page.